THE
IMAGE
OF
MERCY

THE
IMAGE
OF
MERCY

The Most Rev. Emilio S. Allué, S.D.B., D.D.

and

Kathleen Keefe

Peace Through Mercy Publishing
25 Cambridge Avenue
Yonkers, New York 10707
(914)-337-0060   Fax (914) 337-7028

Nihil Obstat: Francis J. McAree, S.T.D., Censor Liborum
Imprimatur: +Patrick J. Sheridan, D.D., Vicar General,
                        Archdiocese of New York
Date: October 4, 1996

First Edition

ISBN: 0-9655231-0-1

All Biblical quotations are from the **New Catholic Study Bible***, St.
Jerome Edition, Catholic Bible Press, 1985.*

Quotations from the Diary of Sr. Faustina M. Kowalska, **Divine Mercy
in My Soul,** *copyright © 1987 Congregation of Marians of the
Immaculate Conception; all world rights reserved; printed with
permission.*

Copies may be obtained from the Publisher:

Peace Through Mercy Publishing
25 Cambridge Avenue
Yonkers, New York 10707
Tel. 914-337-0060   Fax: 914-337-7028

The Authors

The Most Rev. Emilio S. Allué, S.D.B., D.D., Ph.D. is an Auxiliary Bishop of Boston. A Marian theologian, ordained in Rome in 1966, he received his licentiate in Sacred Theology (S.T.L.) in 1967 at Salesian University in Rome and a doctorate (Ph.D.), History of Christianity, from Fordham in 1981.

Born in Huesca, Spain, he entered the Salesian Seminary in 1954. Following first profession, he was assigned to the Salesian Province in New York in 1956. In addition to his native Spanish, Bishop Allué is fluent in English, Italian and French. He has a rich and varied background in priestly formation, teaching, preaching, administration, retreat and pastoral work.

Bishop Allué has been associated with *Peace Through Divine Mercy* since 1993, becoming theological and spiritual advisor to the apostolate in February, 1995.

Kathleen Keefe, a wife, mother and teacher founded *Peace Through Divine Mercy* in 1988, with the support and encouragement of her husband, Martin. An international apostolate for the Renewal of the Priesthood and the Family, it evolved from an act of thanksgiving to the Merciful Jesus after the miraculous healing of one of the Keefe children in 1982.

A native New Yorker, Kathleen is the daughter of Mary and the late Timothy Sullivan, natives of Ireland. A graduate of Fordham University, 1967, B.S. Ed. and the City University of New York, 1971, M.S. Ed., she is a certified counselor, with a background in spiritual direction. She conducts Divine Mercy retreats, parish missions and days of recollection for priests and laity throughout the United States and in Italy. The theme of healing through God's Mercy is central to her work.

Kathleen and Martin were married in 1967 and are the parents of seven children. The entire family has been involved in various aspects of the apostolate since 1988.

The Image of Mercy

In 1992 the Superior General of the Congregation of the Sisters of Our Lady of Mercy in Cracow, Poland gave Kathleen the negative of the miraculous Cracow Image of the Divine Mercy (which is enthroned in the convent's chapel over the tomb of Blessed Faustina), to produce replicas for the apostolate's mission of *Enthronement of the Image of the Divine Mercy* in homes and churches throughout the world.

First Conference on the Apostolic Movement of Divine Mercy
The Shrine of Divine Mercy at Lagiewniki, Cracow, Poland
February 22-24, 1996

At the invitation of Franciszek Cardinal Macharski, Archbishop of Cracow and the Congregation of the Sisters of Our Lady of Mercy, Bishop Emilio Allué and Kathleen Keefe were among 130 representatives of Divine Mercy apostolic movements from 17 nations who met in Poland in February, 1996. The conference opened with Mass celebrated by Cardinal Macharsk and concelebrated by some thirty Bishops and priests who gathered on the 65th anniversary of Blessed Faustina's vision in which Jesus expressed His desire that an image depicting Him as the Merciful Jesus be painted with the signature: *Jesus, I trust in You*. Presentations were made by four Polish Bishops, Sr. Elzbieta Siepak of the Congregation and scholars in biblical and pastoral theology. Calling the Holy Father's encyclical "Dives in Misericordia" the Magna Carta for the movement of Divine Mercy, the Bishops stressed that the Holy Father depends on this cult to rebuild trust in human beings destroyed by sin.

Contents

ENTRUSTMENT

to

Mary Mother of Mercy

whose

Surrender at the Annunciation

brought forth

the gift of

DIVINE MERCY

to the world

"I am Mother to you all thanks to the unfathomable mercy of God. Most pleasing to Me is that soul which faithfully carries out the will of God. Be courageous. Do not fear apparent obstacles, but fix your gaze upon the Passion of My Son, and in this way you will be victorious" **(449)**. *Our Lady to Blessed Faustina*

The Hail Mary

Hail Mary, full of grace. The Lord is with thee; blessed art thou among women, and blessed is the fruit of thy womb, Jesus. Holy Mary, Mother of God, pray for us sinners, now and at the hour of our death. Amen.

INTRODUCTION

The Healing Power of Jesus

I do not remember the first time I saw the Image of the Divine Mercy or how I came to have the little picture in my kitchen back in 1981. I only remember that I was very drawn to it. In 1982, when our sixth child was born, the image took on great significance in our lives. Our son, John, suffered serious complications at birth. For several weeks, his life was in the balance and the prognosis for his future was dismal. As he lay in a neo-natal intensive care unit at a New York hospital, we entrusted his life to the Merciful Jesus whose image we "enthroned" with scotch tape in the most precious spot in our home - his empty crib. In the weeks following his birth, a great outpouring of prayer led to a series of miraculous events that would bring our son home within two weeks. He continued his recovery under the loving gaze of the image of the Divine Mercy.

Because John's early years were plagued by a series of medical problems, we focused on healing prayer. As each difficulty was resolved, we realized that the healing power of Jesus was being released through intercessory prayer and trust, reflected in the praise and thanksgiving we offered in all circumstances, especially when things were not going well. These insights began to transform our lives.

Despite the fact that I was advised by doctors that another pregnancy might result in a similar traumatic birth, God blessed us, once again, with the gift of a beautiful baby girl, Kathleen Keara, born in August 1985.

A Work of the Holy Spirit

By 1987 devotion to the Divine Mercy was an integral par of the life of our family. Supported by my husband and children, the level of my involvement in spreading the message of Divine Mercy increased. With the guidance and encouragement of a priest, who was my spiritual director, I grew in my understanding of the action of the Holy Spirit in my life. God used my background in family counseling to deepen the gifts o healing and discernment of spirits. In association with a Catholic psychiatrist, I gained invaluable experience bringing God's healing to others through prayer, counseling and the gifts of the Holy Spirit. We continually witnessed the power of the Sacraments of Mercy to heal and to set people free from bondage. The combination of the psychological and the spiritual served to reinforce the great power of the sacraments and the priesthood; a power that unfortunately is overlooked by many today.

The Lord continued to send many people who became part of my spiritual journey. One particular blessing was a missionary sister who helped me to understand the spirituality o this new movement. I also worked with many priests in the healing ministry. These practical "hands on" situations gave me the needed experience in pastoral care. This proved to be a prophetic sign of the work the Lord was evolving. The Holy Spirit was leading me to a future that included spiritual direction and retreats for priests. The vision was unfolding, but always in the context of my family and my primary role as wife and mother. I was exposed to a wealth of knowledge and experience while continuing my normal day-to-day activities at home.

The Role of Our Lady

Over a four year period (1987-1991), I traveled with our son, John, to five Marian shrines in Europe, asking Our Lady's help in restoring his health. Her shrines became my classrooms o instruction in the spiritual life. Mary always pointed to her Son, Jesus, in the Eucharist as the source of John's healing. One o many miracles occurred during a pilgrimage to Fatima and

Lourdes in 1989. John had not been able to keep any food in his stomach for almost a month. His undiagnosed digestive illness left him very weak and barely able to travel. Two days into our trip, the priest leading the pilgrimage told me he was convinced that John's health would be restored through the Holy Eucharist. With some preparation (John had the basic instruction), he made his first confession. On the Feast of Our Lady of Mt. Carmel, John received his first Holy Communion at the Basilica of St. Pius X in Lourdes. He was healed the day he received the Holy Eucharist. Doctors could not explain his recovery.

Peace Through Divine Mercy Apostolate

The flow of grace, which began in 1982, was now emerging as a spiritual movement. On the Feast of the Holy Family in 1988, I founded *Peace Through Divine Mercy*. With the blessing and support of the pastor, a small intercessory group began meeting at our parish church every Sunday at the 3 o'clock Hour of Mercy. The image of the Divine Mercy was publicly venerated as the group prayed for families and for priests. We experienced many graces during those days.

Inspired to bring this message in a more personal way to many people, I traveled with three of our children to the Shrine of the Divine Mercy in Cracow, Poland in August 1991. While there, I met with Sister Beata, who had lived with Sister Faustina. I shared with her my vision of having the image enthroned in homes and churches. With her assistance and the blessing of the Superior General of the Congregation of the Sisters of Our Lady of Mercy, the image was dismounted from over the altar at the convent and professionally photographed. The negative of the miraculous *Cracow Image of the Divine Mercy* was given to our family on March 17, 1992. In my heart, the mission of enthronement was confirmed.

Enthronement of the Image of the Divine Mercy in the Home

Since 1992 I have worked with many priests, individuals and families to bring enthronement into homes and parishes. I have witnessed miracles of conversion and healing on a firsthand basis. Jesus' mercy is changing lives in ways that defy human explanation. These miracles heightened my awareness of the forces of evil working in the society to destroy the family and the critical role of the priest in stemming the tide of evil. There are Catholics today as involved as the rest of the population in abortion, contraception and other sins against life, sins against charity and justice, drug abuse, child abuse, occult activities and new age practices. All the evils that plague society, including divorce, have penetrated the sanctity of the Catholic home. Our families are desperately crying out for help and the Merciful Jesus has given us the help to restore peace in our lives and in our homes - His Divine Mercy. By enthroning the King of Mercy in the home, we invite Jesus to restore the sanctity of our home and the dignity of each person.

Our work of enthronement is part of the apostolate's mission of priestly and family renewal. **Priests of the Enthronement** and **Families of the Enthronement** bring the urgent message of Divine Mercy to the world.

Priests of the Enthronement are loyal sons of Mary who understand the need to proclaim mercy in these days of darkness and confusion. They are readily identifiable, for Jesus has singled them out for extraordinary blessings: *"To priests who proclaim and extol My mercy, I will give wondrous power; I will anoint their words and touch the hearts of those to whom they will speak"* (1521).

Families of the Enthronement are those families who have welcomed the King of Mercy into their homes and now share the blessings of enthronement with other families. Jesus promised: *"With souls that have recourse to My mercy and with those that glorify and proclaim My great mercy to others, I will* *deal according to My infinite mercy at the hour of their death"* (379).

Youth of the Enthronement is a dream yet to be realized. Young people must also be involved in the work of enthroning Jesus, King of Mercy.

Divine Mercy Priests' Retreat Ministry

The vision continued to unfold. One year after the work of enthronement began, I entered more deeply into the heart of the work of the apostolate - priestly renewal. In every way this has been the greatest challenge. For five years the work of priestly renewal was concentrated on intercessory prayer for priests and promoting devotion to the Divine Mercy among priests. In 1993, it expanded to include a retreat ministry to priests. While en route to Rome with a group of pilgrims, we visited San Giovanni Rotondo, where Padre Pio lived out his victim priesthood and is now buried. Many healings took place during our brief visit, two involving priests. On the eve of the beatification of Sister Faustina, Fr. Joseph Pius Martin, O.F.M.Cap., asked me to establish a retreat ministry to priests at San Giovanni Rotondo. *Divine Mercy Priests' Retreats*, honoring the Eucharistic Heart of Jesus, was born in the shadow of the Gargano Mountain under the protection of Our Lady of Grace and her faithful priest son, Padre Pio. The years of quiet preparation had taken root.

The first priests' retreat was held in Italy in July 1994. It was funded, for the most part, by the "hidden apostles" who carry out the work of spreading the Divine Mercy devotion. In a matter of six weeks, a small group of friends raised enough money to hold the retreat, which was attended by seventeen American priests. Since that time, priests from many different parts of the world have expressed a desire to attend the retreats. Hopefully, generous benefactors will come forward to establish a foundation for priestly renewal to ensure that the *Divine Mercy Priests Retreats* continue in San Giovanni Rotondo. Such a foundation would also make it possible to hold the retreats in the United States as well as other countries.

The first Spanish language *Divine Mercy Priests' Retreat* was conducted in Honduras in October 1995. There is nothing more important, in my view, than the work of priestly renewal. It is inextricably linked to family renewal. Without our priests to nourish our spiritual lives through the sacraments, great darkness will descend upon our families and our entire world. My prayer is that many will be moved to support our efforts in every way possible.

In 1995, a lay retreat ministry, *Rebuild My Church*, was founded in San Giovanni Rotondo, to work and pray for priestly and family renewal. These retreats will be conducted here in the United States as well as in other countries.

A New Apostolate Bringing Renewal Through Divine Mercy

In the following pages you will be introduced to the theology and spirituality of a new apostolate of mercy for these times. *Peace Through Divine Mercy's* apostolic work of renewal and evangelization has evolved as the vision has materialized. The spirituality of the apostolate is intimately connected with its work of renewal. This is the reason that we encourage individuals and families to embrace the spiritual practices of the apostolate, most of which are based on devotion to the Divine Mercy, in order to derive the maximum benefits from enthronement in the home and parish.

The first part of the book lays the foundation of the apostolate and supports the urgent need for priestly and family renewal, through the *Divine Mercy Priests' Retreat Ministry* and the work of **Enthronement of the Image of the Divine Mercy** throughout the world. The second part of the book details the **Nine Graces of Enthronement of the Image of the Divine Mercy in the Home.** It concludes with the *Rite of Enthronement* and the **Act of Consecration of the Family to the Merciful Jesus.** The graces are not limited to those mentioned in the work. However, they do represent the key areas of healing and restoration we have witnessed in families since the work of *Enthronement* began in 1992. You will notice that there is a great emphasis on healing. Each of us, our families, our priests and religious, are in need of God's healing. We are all wounded and broken in a society whose moral values continue to decline. Jesus said to Sister Faustina: *"I do not want to punish aching mankind, but I desire to heal it, pressing it to My Merciful Heart"* (1588). My hope is that we respond while there is still time.

We invite you to become part of this grassroots movement of mercy. Through many "hidden apostles" who have answered "yes" to Jesus' call to be merciful as He is merciful, this person-to-person and family-to-family apostolate continues its spread throughout the United States as well as in various parts of the world where it has been introduced through the efforts of *Apostles of Divine Mercy.*

Kathleen Keefe

ACKNOWLEDGMENTS

I thank Almighty God and my beloved Mother Mary for the gift of Divine Mercy. Blessed Faustina, I thank you for your presence as a sister to me.

My heartfelt love and gratitude to my husband, Martin, whose love, sacrifices, quiet strength and constant support enabled me to develop the vision; and to our seven children, whose love and understanding made it possible for me to be clay in the hands of the potter. I thank all of my family for their love and support, especially my dear mother, Mary Sullivan, whose life is a constant prayer. My love and gratitude to all my friends who have prayed, sacrificed and believed in this work of God's mercy from its inception.

I am grateful to the Merciful Jesus for my spiritual directors; our first national chaplain, Fr. Dominick Morrissette, God's instrument of healing through the Holy Eucharist; Sister Reina Paz, M.M. whose encouragement and insights from that "first day" we met in 1987 have been realized in the writing of this book; Sr. Mary Ann Follmar, Dominican theologian from Providence College who has been a great inspiration to me; George Hogben, M.D., who has given so generously of his time and talent in advancing the work of the apostolate; the Sisters of Bethlehem, who have prayed for this mission since their arrival in New York in 1987; the Archdiocese of New York, for its blessing on this Divine Mercy apostolate and on its work of evangelization.

My heartfelt gratitude to Fr. Joseph Pius Martin, O.F.M.Cap. of the Capuchin Friary at San Giovanni Rotondo Italy, whose vision and trust in God made the *Divine Mercy Priests' Retreats* a reality. I thank Fr. Bernard Bush, S.J. of Los Altos, Ca., who co-directed the first retreat in Italy, giving so much of himself to the work of priestly renewal.

A very special thank you to Archbishop Gabriel Gonsum Ganaka of Jos, Nigeria, President of the Episcopal Conference of

Africa and Madagascar, for leading us in our first public Act of Consecration as Apostles of Divine Mercy, in the Church of the Holy Spirit, the Shrine Church of the Divine Mercy in Rome, in May, 1995. It was an extraordinary blessing.

I am grateful to Father Glenn Sudano, C.F.R., who co-directed our first lay apostles retreat in Italy.

My deepest gratitude to you, Most Rev. Francisco Garmendia, D.D., Auxiliary Bishop of New York, for your friendship, encouragement and example as a zealous apostle of God's Mercy. You have brought the Mercy of Jesus to so many souls and *Enthronement* to so many homes and churches.

I thank Mother Helena Paulina, Superior General of the Congregation that gave Blessed Faustina Kowalska of the Most Blessed Sacrament to the world and Sister Beata for your kindness and generosity toward me. The gift of the negative of the miraculous Cracow Image of the Divine Mercy is a sacred trust that encourages us in our mission to *"...let every soul have access to it"* (570).

I went to Poland in 1991 with a dream and a mission. You, Mother Paulina, helped both to be realized when you responded to the request of a grateful mother. The fruit of your generosity is the work of Enthronement of the Image of the Divine Mercy in homes and churches throughout the world.

My heartfelt gratitude to you, Most Rev. Emilio S. Allué, S.D.B., D.D., our faithful friend. Your personal involvement in all aspects of the apostolate since 1993 has contributed to our growth and emergence as a new apostolate of mercy and renewal. In co-authoring this book, you have advanced the work of priestly and family renewal, particularly through the apostolate's mission of *Enthronement* and the *Divine Mercy Priests' Retreat Ministry*. Your unfailing commitment to proclaiming the Mercy of God will continue to bear great fruit to the farthest ends of the earth.

Bishop Allué and I are deeply grateful to the generous benefactor who made it possible to publish this book.

The Cracow Image of the Divine Mercy

The front cover of the book is a canvas reproduction of the Cracow Image of the Divine Mercy produced from the negative given to our family in 1992 by the Congregation of the Sisters of Our Lady of Mercy in Poland.

The beautiful replica of the image as well as the color enhancement of Blessed Faustina, are the work of our daughter, Mary Kate, who has given so generously of her time, talent and heart to this mission. The technical assistance of my husband, Martin, and the expertise of my brother, artist, Edmund Sullivan, completed the effort. This framed reproduction (copyright 1992) is the one enthroned in churches. Smaller reproductions, as well as the large canvas reproduction, are available for home enthronement.

The first "print" reproduction of the Cracow Image of the Divine Mercy was enthroned in the Church of St. Thomas Aquinas in the Bronx, New York by the pastor, The Most Reverend Francisco Garmendia, Auxiliary Bishop of New York, with whom I am privileged to work in spreading devotion to the Divine Mercy in New York.

The first "canvas" reproduction of the Cracow Image was enthroned in our own parish Church of the Annunciation, Yonkers, New York on September 8, 1992 by our pastor, Msgr. James R. Moore. It was at Annunciation that the seed was planted and first supported by our former pastor, Fr. James Conte, who blessed our Sunday Divine Mercy Holy Hours in 1988. I am grateful for two wonderful, supportive pastors.

The Apostolate's reproductions are now in churches and homes throughout the United States, and abroad.

Chapter 1

DIVINE MERCY

"Paint an image according to the pattern you see, with the signature: Jesus, I trust in You. I desire that this image be venerated, first in your chapel and [then] throughout the world" (Diary, 47).

THE DIVINE MERCY DEVOTION

The *essence* of the Divine Mercy devotion is **TRUST**. It is the vessel for drawing the graces of God's Mercy. *"If their trust is great, there is no limit to My generosity,"* Jesus said (1602).* Accordingly, Jesus wants us to ask for an abundance of treasures; He waits to give them to us. Jesus, who delights in a soul's trust, keeps that soul in His personal care.

In addition, the attitude of mercy toward one's neighbor is necessary for obtaining graces. Jesus gave us three ways of exercising this mercy toward our neighbor: by deed, by word and by prayer. These three degrees embody the fullness of God's mercy. Jesus calls them a proof of our love for Him. The practice of mercy is clearly a condition for receiving God's Mercy.

The Forms of the Devotion to the Divine Mercy are:

- **The Image of the Divine Mercy**

- **The Feast of Mercy**

- **The Chaplet of the Divine Mercy**

- **The Hour of Mercy**

---

* Diary entry numbers printed after each quotation are from the *Diary of Sister Faustina M. Kowalska, Divine Mercy in My Soul.*

The Image of the Divine Mercy

Jesus appeared to Sister Faustina in a vision on February 22, 1931. He expressed His desire that an image be painted with the signature, *Jesus, I Trust in You.* The representation is that of the risen Christ, with hands and feet bearing the marks of the crucifixion. From His pierced Heart, not visible in the image, two rays issue forth. Jesus explained that the pale rays represent the *Water which makes souls righteous* and the red rays represent the *Blood which is the life of souls (299).*

The image portrays the Merciful Jesus. It is the vessel Jesus offers us in order that we continue to come for graces to the fountain of mercy. The image is a reminder to the world of the demands of God's mercy and the absolute necessity to practice works of mercy.

Jesus promised that those who venerated His sacred image with trust, exercising mercy in deed, word and prayer, would receive the grace of salvation, great progress on the road to Christian perfection and the grace of a happy death.

The Feast of Mercy

The Feast of Mercy is celebrated on the first Sunday after Easter. On this day we contemplate the Mystery of Redemption as the greatest revelation of Divine Mercy towards us. It is a day of extraordinary grace for those who are in the state of grace, having made a good confession during the lenten period preceding the Feast. The faithful must fulfill the conditions of the Divine Mercy devotion (trust and active love of neighbor), and receive Holy Communion on the Feast of Mercy. Those who are not familiar with the devotion or sinners who are converted on the Feast of Mercy receive the graces and blessings promised by Jesus when they fulfill the obligation of a good confession and worthy reception of the Holy Eucharist. Jesus said: *"The souls that will go to confession and receive Holy Communion shall obtain complete forgiveness of sins and punishment"* (699).

Jesus asked that the Feast of Mercy be preceded by a novena of chaplets, for nine days, beginning on Good Friday. Our Lord promised to grant souls all possible graces through this novena. The novena may also be said at any other time of the year.

At the celebration of the Feast of Mercy the image of the Divine Mercy is to be solemnly blessed and publicly venerated. Priests are to speak to souls about the Mercy of God on this day. Jesus called the Feast *"a refuge and shelter for all souls, and especially for poor sinners"* (699).

The Chaplet of the Divine Mercy

Our Lord dictated this prayer to Sister Faustina in 1935. It is said on ordinary rosary beads and is a prayer in which we offer to God the Father "the Body and Blood, Soul and Divinity" of Jesus Christ in an act of atonement for our sins and the sins of the world. The chaplet is a very powerful prayer for the dying (811, 1797); for the conversion of sinners (687); to obtain special graces and favors (1541); to appease God's anger (476); to avert natural disasters (474, 1128); and to dispel the attacks of the evil one (1798). It is to be prayed in a spirit of trust and humility. Jesus said: *"By saying the chaplet you are bringing humankind closer to me"* (929). Jesus made it clear that He was giving the chaplet to the whole world and that extraordinary graces were attached to its recitation. *"Through the chaplet you will obtain everything, if what you ask for is compatible with My will"* (1731). The chaplet is especially efficacious at the hour of death when Our Lord promised great mercy to those who pray the chaplet, and for the dying at whose bedside others say this prayer.

The Hour of Mercy

Jesus asked that we implore His mercy for the entire world, and especially for sinners, at the hour of three o'clock. We are asked to immerse ourselves in His Passion and appeal to the merits of His bitter Passion, even if only for a moment. This meditation brings us into the mystery of the Cross," *"the hour of grace for the whole world-mercy triumphed over justice"* (1572). Jesus requested that Sister Faustina make the Stations of the Cross in this hour, if her duties permitted. If not, He asked that she visit Him in the Blessed Sacrament and adore His heart *"which is full of mercy"* (1572). He further suggested that if this were not possible, *"immerse yourself in prayer there where you happen to be, if only for a very brief instant"* (1572).

Spreading Devotion to the Divine Mercy

Jesus promised special protection for those who propagate His mercy. *"Souls who spread the honor of My mercy I shield through their entire lives as a tender mother her infant, and at the hour of death I will not be a Judge for them, but the Merciful Savior"* (1075). Jesus also said: *"...they will not experience terror at the hour of death; My mercy will shield them in that final battle"* (1540). Priests who speak about God's unfathomable mercy and compassion are assured that *"hardened sinners will repent on hearing their words"* (1521).

THE SACRAMENTS OF MERCY

HOLY EUCHARIST

On the night before His bitter Passion and death, Jesus gave Himself to us in the Holy Eucharist, His Body and Blood, Soul and Divinity. In an act of total surrender, He gave us the gift of perfect love, that we might have at every Mass, the unbloody sacrifice of Calvary. Only when we eat His Body, allowing Jesus total access to our hearts, can we understand the meaning of love. This gift of mercy continues the loving and healing presence of Jesus in our lives today. It is God's covenant of love in which He comes to be present within us each time we receive Him in Holy Communion.

Throughout history, chosen souls have been called by God to bring urgent messages to wounded mankind. Through His servant, Sister Faustina, the Merciful Jesus affirms His living presence in the Eucharist and convicts us of our indifference toward Him in the Blessed Sacrament. *"Oh, how painful it is to Me that souls so seldom unite themselves to Me in Holy Communion. I wait for souls, and they are indifferent toward Me. I love them tenderly and sincerely, and they distrust Me. I want to lavish My graces on them, and they do not want to accept them..."* (1447). Our Lord graced Sister Faustina with many visions during her daily Mass and at the time of Holy Communion. *"Oh, what awesome mysteries take place during Mass! One day we will know what God is doing for us in each Mass,"* wrote Sister Faustina (914). This emphasis on the Eucharist and the Holy Sacrifice of the Mass is particularly relevant in these times when many have lost belief in the true presence and no longer understand the meaning of the Mass.

THE SACRAMENT OF RECONCILIATION

The Sacrament of Reconciliation brings the mercy of God to our souls through the forgiveness of our sins. It is a sacrament of healing and mercy where Jesus says *"the greatest miracles take place [and] are incessantly repeated."* Sister Faustina wrote: *"The miracle of Divine Mercy restores the soul in full"* (1448). The words of Our Lord give us valuable information about our healing, the role of the priest, our attitude as we approach the Sacrament and the action of grace in the soul.

In this sacrament, we accept Jesus as the divine healer, the divine counselor, the crucified Savior and Redeemer. Jesus stressed that He is the one who acts in the soul of the penitent. *"When the priest acts in my place, he does not act of himself, but I act through him. His wishes are mine"* (331).

The words of Our Lord teach us anew about the graces available to us in this sacrament. Jesus also provides teaching to the priest who is confessor and spiritual director. He confirms the great gift of the priesthood and the extraordinary power He has given to priests to touch even the most hardened of sinners.

Chapter 2

PEACE THROUGH DIVINE MERCY APOSTOLATE

"To Restore All Things in Christ"
Pope St. Pius X

Peace Through Divine Mercy Apostolate

Mission Statement

Peace Through Divine Mercy Apostolate seeks to evangelize in the world by means of the Gospel message of *Divine Mercy*. Such evangelization is to effect religious renewal in *families*, in the *priesthood* and *religious life* through the sacramental life of the Church and in particular through deepening our appreciation of the healing power of the Sacraments of Reconciliation and Holy Eucharist.

To accomplish this, **Peace Through Divine Mercy:**

- Promotes *Enthronement of the Image of the Divine Mercy* in homes and churches, and *Consecration of the Family to the Merciful Jesus*, encouraging the spread of devotion to the Divine Mercy in all its aspects.

- Conducts *Divine Mercy Priests' Retreats* to affirm our priests and renew in them the mystery of the priestly vocation by helping priests experience the companionship of Jesus, and their configuration to Him, especially Christ crucified and risen.

- Forms *Apostles of Divine Mercy* to uphold the ministerial priesthood of Jesus Christ and work for the renewal of families through the Divine Mercy.

A New Apostolate of Mercy

Apostles of These Times

Peace Through Divine Mercy is a movement of the Holy Spirit, building up the kingdom of Grace and Mercy within human hearts and spreading God's mercy in the world. It responds to our need for inner peace and personal wholeness through God's mercy. This movement challenges us to build the Kingdom of Jesus in our spiritual lives. Its spirituality is based on the Divine Life and the healing power of Jesus through His Word and sacraments. **Peace Through Divine Mercy** relies solely on the presence of the Holy Spirit empowering us in our renewal and growth in holiness and in active charity. Once renewed, we live in the grace of God and grow in real inner peace and love.

The unique aspect of this apostolate consists in its personal approach to God's mercy through conversion and healing. Conversion, if it is to bear fruit, must lead to true repentance. True repentance, in turn, leads to apostolic fervor. With our faith strengthened, we are led by grace to change our attitudes and actions, especially through the practice of mercy and forgiveness toward ourselves and our neighbor. The Word of God and constant prayer in the Spirit transform our souls into living channels of mercy and peace. As we are immersed in God's mercy, we become *Apostles of Divine Mercy*, modern messengers of that very mercy incarnated in Jesus Christ.

Peace Through Divine Mercy, initiated by the Holy Spirit in its founder, follows the mission of the Church in the evangelization of peoples and cultures. Its evangelization efforts aim at reanimating, with a sense of confident hope, the priestly powers of a renewed clergy and laity (families), operating always with and by the Word and Sacrament of the Merciful Jesus. With humble and confident hearts, we, *Apostles of Divine Mercy*, depend on the active presence of our ever loving and merciful Mother of God, Help of all Christians and Star of the New Evangelization.

Theological Vision

God is the "Father of mercies," the author of life, and by a special act of His Will, creator of our human race. From the beginning of creation, when the human race became prey to the evil one, God Himself worked His plan of salvation and grace. He selected and guided a chosen people through the centuries of the Old Testament. He doted on them with infinite compassion and mercy and rescued them from all their infidelities. God's mercy flowed to them from His infinite love and fidelity to His covenant. His Goodness as a Father reached out to His children with fatherly tenderness.

In the Incarnation of the Son of God, mankind received the fullness of His love through the Passion, Death and Resurrection of Jesus Christ. The Paschal Mysteries bring about the redemption of all men and women who, being reconciled with the Father, are now endowed with the Divine Life. This harmony with the creator constitutes real and lasting peace. The word "shalom" clearly indicates this reality of total well-being and complete union with the Will of the Father. It is the fullness of life lived according to God's Law. The agent of this lasting peace is Jesus Himself, the Prince of Peace, who gives His Peace to all who receive His Word and sacraments.

PEACE: Conformity to the Divine Will

The ministry of **Peace Through Divine Mercy** embraces the PEACE that is fulfilled in Jesus Christ. The basis of this peace lies in conformity of our human will to the Divine Will. This inner conformity produces a deep sense of happiness and joy, which is in direct contrast to the power of evil manifested through sin. Jesus' mercy overpowers any influence of the devil, healing any kind of separation from God caused by the presence of sin. Peace and happiness overcome agitation, misery and the state of brokenness. The words of Jesus, "Go in peace," restored the health of the body and signified victory over sin and the power of the devil.

The Peace that Christ offers is the product of justice and charity lived according to God's Will. Justice consists in the firm and constant will to give God and our neighbor their due. Charity is to love God above all things and our neighbor as ourselves for love of God. Charity, the form of all virtues, **"binds everything together in perfect harmony"** -Col. 3:14. To the extent that we are not in conformity to the Divine Will, peace is lacking in our hearts and in the world.

Sacraments of Mercy (Healing)

In the ever present struggle with the evil powers of sin and death, Jesus' love and mercy impart strength and wisdom and communicate the power of His Spirit. In His Sacraments of Mercy, the Eucharist and Reconciliation, our souls are touched and healed. Jesus, Mercy Itself, is the only one at the center in the long and challenging pilgrimage to the Father. He is the Mediator who, in a new Eternal Priesthood, surpasses the old priesthood of the Mosaic law. His Peace is actualized today through His priesthood which He shares with His faithful (the common priesthood of the laity), and especially with His ordained priests (the ministerial priesthood).

The mercy (love) of God needs a priesthood restored in harmony and in unity with Jesus' priesthood. His divine mercy brings healing to the priest and gives focus to the direction and ministerial mission required in these times of confusion and insecurity. The same merciful love of the Father brings healing to the hearts of the faithful in order to recreate in them the restoration and practice of their faith.

The Holy Spirit

At the heart of this movement is a merciful Father who loves us to the extreme of sending His Son to become one of us in everything but sin, offering Him as a Victim of expiation. Mary, full of grace, was chosen from all ages to bring forth the Redeemer in a spotless and pure way. The overshadowing of the Holy Spirit made it possible for the Word to become flesh. As the

Spouse of Mary, the Holy Spirit gives birth to Jesus the Savior in His human life. This same Spirit is manifested at Pentecost as He gives birth to the new people of God, the Church. The third person of the Holy Trinity is ever present and active from the beginning of creation.

In our times, the Holy Spirit continues the work of restoration and sanctification of the human soul, inspiring in it a strong faith, a trusting hope and a loving charity in total submission to God's Will. Thus, the powerful agent of the soul's conversion to God and immersion in His merciful Heart is the Holy Spirit sent by Jesus Himself.

Mary, Mother of Mercy and Help of Christians

The loving presence of Mary, Mother of Mercy and Help of all Christians is a vital part of this movement. In the Incarnation of the Son of God and in the work of redemption on the Cross, Mary was an active participant and cooperator. As the Sorrowful Mother, Mary played an important and unique role in obtaining for mankind the Father's eternal, merciful love. By express mandate of her Son on the Cross, she became the Mother of the Church for all generations to come. Ever since that "new birth," Mary has exercised her motherhood of grace and mercy. She has shown her loving kindness as the real Mother of life, mercy and grace. She is the Queen of Peace who brought to the world the Prince of Peace.

In Mary's role as intercessor on our behalf, she leads the Church to the Father through Jesus Christ. Her power is that of her Son, as she helps in the conversion of sinners and the protection and renewal of the Body of Christ. As mother of priests and helper of all Christians, she inspires a sense of hope and trust, joy and peace. With her chaste spouse, Joseph, Mary places Jesus at the center of today's families, renewing and healing them.

Apostles of Divine Mercy

We, *Apostles of Divine Mercy*, comprised of renewed priests, consecrated souls and committed laity become victims of reparation for ourselves and the whole world. We take part in our own renewal in an interaction of prayerful support and love. Our efforts in spreading the work of Divine Mercy are rekindled by coming into contact with the Eucharistic Lord, reception of the Sacraments of Mercy, constant prayer to Jesus and Mary and meditation on the Word of God. Closely associated with these practices are personal ongoing formation as well as personal enrichment and inspiration through the writings of the saints, in particular, Blessed Faustina. Relying on these divine agents of mercy: Jesus, the Holy Spirit and Holy Mary, we, *Apostles of Divine Mercy* live our total consecration to God with peace and joy.

Total Consecration to Jesus Through Mary

United in faith and trusting in the Merciful Jesus, the **Apostles of Peace Through Divine Mercy** are involved in the Church's mission of spreading the Mercy of God. Our growth in holiness demands a total consecration to Jesus through His Mother Mary. In our Marian and Eucharistic piety, we are conscious that our person and possessions are offered to Jesus through Mary. A "Totus Tuus" mentality is critical in our growth as committed *Apostles of Divine Mercy*.

Chapter 3

Spirituality of
The Apostles of
Peace Through Divine Mercy

"I want you to become like a knight experienced in battle, who can give orders to others amid the exploding shells. In the same way, My child, you should know how to master yourself amid the greatest difficulties, and let nothing drive you away from Me, not even your falls" (Diary 1823).

Spirituality
of
the Apostles of
Peace Through Divine Mercy

The spirituality of **Peace Through Divine Mercy** stresses:

- **A personal relationship with the Merciful Jesus,** who wishes to form us in the way of peace, love and mercy. Christ's peace is realized in our lives when we embrace His mercy. Touched by love, we become channels of peace in our families, our communities and in the world. Our personal relationship with Jesus is enhanced through meditation on the Paschal mysteries, particularly His sorrowful Passion and death.

This apostolate relies on the Holy Spirit to move our spirits to walk in the way of peace and to act in and through the power of the Holy Spirit. The fruit of acting in the Holy Spirit is **obedience to the Word of God.** Jesus, who is the Way, the Truth and the Life said: **"If you obey my teaching, you are really my disciples; you will know the truth and the truth will set you free "** -John 8:31. This emphasis on obedience and discipleship is key to our understanding of truth.

- **Obedience and forgiveness** are interconnected. When we obey God, we are in union with Him. When we disobey God, we must seek His forgiveness in order to restore ourselves to a right relationship with Him. The more we fail to obey the Word of God, the farther we flee from His forgiveness. In not seeking God's forgiveness through repentance and reconciliation, we increase the likelihood of being unable to forgive ourselves and others. We have altered the flow of God's love and mercy in our lives. Unforgiveness, which is at the root of much of the suffering in families and in the world, robs us of the Peace of Christ. The **Sacrament of**

Reconciliation, which Jesus called, *"the tribunal of My mercy,"* (975) restores the Peace of Christ in our lives and gives us the grace to live in obedience to the Will of God.

- **The Holy Eucharist** is the source of our life and our healing. The spirituality of this movement is rooted in the Eucharistic Heart of Jesus and stresses belief in the living presence of Jesus in the Eucharist, worthy reception of the Holy Eucharist and Eucharistic adoration.

The spirituality of **Peace Through Divine Mercy** concentrates on one's individual encounter with God and the importance of entering into the grace of the moment. This encounter is a critical juncture on our earthly pilgrimage. It is the moment of Truth when we surrender everything to the Hearts of Jesus and Mary, seeking the graces we need to be renewed and restored. It is the moment we are confronted with our own vulnerability and sinfulness; the moment of grace accepted or rejected. It is the moment when Truth reveals what is in the storehouse of our hearts. And always, amidst our struggles, "His Mercy endures forever" (Ps. 136). This is the great grace of conversion; the Holy Spirit convicting our consciences and calling us to *peace, healing and reconciliation*. It is the moment of grace that begins our journey as *Apostles of Divine Mercy*.

As apostles, it is our daily witness of trust in God and mercy toward our neighbor that proclaims God's mercy in the world. We are called to the exercise of mercy toward our neighbor by deed, word and prayer in the ordinary circumstances of daily life. Turning to the Heavenly Father, we offer Him the Person of the Son of God Incarnate. Invoking the sorrowful Passion of Jesus, each of us make reparation for our sins and the sins of the whole world. We plead for Jesus' Mercy which He wishes to bestow on us and on the whole world.

Apostles of Divine Mercy **turn** to the Merciful Jesus as the source of love and healing. We **open** the door of our hearts to Jesus and **trust** in His love and mercy. We **acknowledge** our total dependence on Him, which helps us to grow in our **love** of God and neighbor. Repenting of our sins and turning away from all that leads to sin, enables us to become living channels of mercy in the **TOTAL** giving of ourselves to Jesus.

As apostles we embrace Mary, Mother of Mercy, living in her Sorrowful and Immaculate Heart. Mary, Help of Christians is our sure refuge as we implore her to "pray for us sinners, now and at the hour of our death." Our spirituality is Eucharistic and Marian.

Our Lady of Guadalupe
"the Merciful Mother of all mankind"
Our Lady to Blessed Juan Diego (Dec. 9, 1531)

"Mother of the Church....we wish to be entirely yours and to walk with you along the way of complete faithfulness to Jesus Christ in His Church: hold us always with your loving hand."

Pope John Paul ll
Basilica of Our Lady of Guadalupe
January 27, 1989

THE ROLE OF
MARY, MOTHER OF MERCY

The spirituality of the apostolate has evolved under the guidance of the Holy Spirit and Mary, Mother of Mercy. Mary has led us to understand our mission as apostles in these times. The following is a brief summary of her role in our apostolate.

As **Mother of Mercy**, Mary intercedes for us before the throne of the King of Mercy. She is the dispenser of the graces of Mercy, and the tenderhearted Mother of all mankind. **Mary, Help of Christians** leads us to her Son in the Holy Eucharist. **Mary, Reconciler**, moves us to repentance and reconciliation. The Mother of Mercy, who has given the world the Divine Mercy, urgently calls her children into the Merciful Heart of Jesus to be healed, renewed and restored. She is the Mother of Life.

As **Mother of the Enthronement** she leads us to enthrone the King of Mercy in our homes and consecrate our families to her Son, Jesus. By enthroning the image of the King of Mercy, Mary, Mother and Queen of Mercy becomes Mother of the Family.

As **Mother of God** she leads us to Total Consecration to her Son, Jesus, thus giving birth to the reign of Jesus in our souls. It is she who teaches us to pray the mysteries of the Rosary from the heart.

As **Mother of Carmel** she invites us to clothe ourselves in her garment, the Brown Scapular of Our Lady of Mt. Carmel, as a pledge of our love and fidelity and acceptance of her special protection against the forces of evil.

As **Mother of Priests** she forms us as intercessors to uphold the ministerial priesthood of her Son, Jesus Christ, through daily prayer and sacrifice. By grace, we receive a deeper understanding of the gift of the priesthood. She revealed to

Sister Faustina that she was *"...the Mother of God of Priests"* (1585).

As **Mother and Teacher of the Faith and First Evangelist**, she has the unique role of forming us in truth and leading us to sanctity. In this way, Mary, spouse of the Holy Spirit and Mother of the Church dispenses the graces that enable us to be faithful to the teachings of her Son, Jesus Christ and to the Magisterium of the Church. Pope John Paul II prayed before the tilma: "Mother of the Church,...we wish to be entirely yours and to walk with you along the way of complete faithfulness to Jesus Christ in His Church; hold us always with your loving hand."

Mary, First Evangelist

Mary, our Mother, is the perfect disciple and the first evangelist. Three important moments in her life provide the example we strive to imitate as *Apostles of Divine Mercy:*

THE ANNUNCIATION
First, we imitate Mary's "yes"

Apostles of Divine Mercy answer "yes" in imitation of Mary at the Annunciation. Turning to God, we open our hearts, in a spirit of humility, inviting the Holy Spirit into our lives. This act of trust is our acceptance of God's Mercy. Jesus Himself invites us to immerse ourselves in His Divine Mercy and to receive it completely.

LET IT BE DONE ACCORDING TO YOUR WILL
Second, we surrender to the Divine Will

The second example we strive to imitate is surrender to the Divine Will. Surrender is the fruit of a humble contrite heart that acknowledges total dependence on the Merciful Jesus as Savior, Redeemer, Healer and Source of everlasting life.

Transformation (conversion) is a gift of God's Mercy. Jesus effects in our souls, through His Holy Spirit, the graces necessary for renewal. Obedience and submission to the Will of God release the power of the Holy Spirit, enabling us to share God's love and mercy with greater freedom of spirit. Witnessing to God's mercy breaks down walls of resistance in us and in our neighbor. To the degree that we surrender to the Divine Will, our souls experience the flames of mercy burning within our hearts. In turn, we pour out the flames of mercy upon other souls. As apostles, we give birth to Jesus, in imitation of Mary, in the hearts of those to whom we bring the Merciful Jesus.

THE VISITATION
Third, we respond to the call

This is our call to action as apostles. St. Luke connects the Annunciation to the Visitation by saying that Mary went to see Elizabeth "in those days." Elizabeth was in her sixth month of pregnancy. Mary went in haste to visit Elizabeth and be of help to her. Mary responded with a heart of mercy. Thus, our Mother became the first missionary carrying the One who comes to renew the face of the earth - our Savior and Redeemer.

In the encounter of Mary with Elizabeth we witness the manifestation of Jesus living in Mary through the power of the Holy Spirit; the same Spirit that made it possible for Elizabeth to "see" with the eyes of faith. The leaping of the future Baptizer is indicative of the great joy that mankind experiences at the incarnation of its Savior.

Blessed Sister Faustina Kowalska
of the Most Blessed Sacrament
1905-1938

Apostle and "Secretary of Divine Mercy"

"Her mission continues and is bearing surprising fruits. It is truly wonderful how her devotion to merciful Jesus is making headway in the contemporary world and conquering so many human hearts! This is undoubtedly a sign of the times, a sign of our twentieth century.

Where then, if not in Divine Mercy, can the world find the safety and light of hope? Believers understand this perfectly!"

John Paul II
Homily -April 18, 1993
Beatification of Sr. Faustina

It began with the healing of a child...

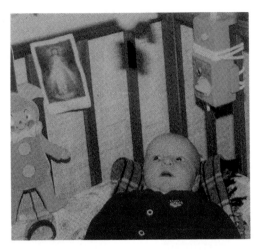

1982-Yonkers, New York. John Keefe at two months. The image of the Divine Mercy was taped to his crib during the time family and friends prayed for his healing.

1989-Lourdes, France. John Keefe, 6, was healed of a serious digestive disorder after receiving his First Holy Communion at Lourdes on the Feast of Our Lady of Mount Carmel.

1992-Santa Maria, Ca. Kathleen Keefe presents the
apostolate's first replica of the Cracow image. The July
4th events highlighted the role of Our Lady of Guadalupe,
Mother of Mercy, who gave birth to the Merciful Jesus and
brings to us the apostolic work of Enthronement of the
"King of Mercy" in homes and churches.

1993-Cracow, Poland. Mother Miriam, then Superior in
Cracow, accepts the apostolate's replica of the Cracow
image. The replica, from the negative of the Hyla painting,
was given to Kathleen by Mother General Helena Paulina
for the mission of Enthronement.

"From Poland will come forth the spark that will prepare the world for My final coming" (Diary, 1732).

Blessed Faustina of the Most Blessed Sacrament

"It is only in eternity that we shall know the great mystery effected in us by Holy Communion. O most precious moments of life" (Diary, 840).

April 18, 1993-Rome-Beatification of Sr. Faustina. Pope John Paul II giving the Holy Eucharist to Kathleen Keefe, 7, at the Beatification. She is the youngest of the seven children of Kathleen and Martin Keefe.

Divine Mercy Priests' Retreat Ministry
San Giovanni Rotondo
1994

Fr. Joseph Pius Martin, O.F.M.Cap. and Kathleen Keefe
prepare for the first *Divine Mercy Priests' Retreat*. Father
Joseph, a member of the retreat team, has spent his entire
priesthood in San Giovanni Rotondo. He shares his personal
memories of Padre Pio, his mission and spirituality.

Priests attending the retreat concelebrate the Holy
Sacrifice of the Mass near the crypt where Padre Pio
is buried.

Divine Mercy Priests' Retreat Ministry

1994-San Giovanni Rotondo, Italy. Co-directors, Fr. Bernard J. Bush, S.J. and Kathleen Keefe, join a group of priests at sunrise for *the Way of the Cross. The Divine Mercy Priests' Retreat Ministry* was established by Fr. Joseph Pius Martin, O.F.M.,Cap. and Kathleen Keefe in the town made famous by the priest-victim Padre Pio.

1995-Honduras. Bishop Gerald Scarpone, O.F.M. and the priests of the Diocese of Comayagua at the first Spanish language *Divine Mercy Priests' Retreat* preached by Bishop Emilio Allué.

Divine Mercy Lay Retreat Ministry

1995-Rome. Archbishop Gabriel Gonsum Ganaka, Jos, Nigeria, President of the Symposium of Episcopal Conferences of Africa and Madagascar, (inset) led the apostolate's lay retreatants in an Act of Consecration as *Apostles of Divine Mercy.* The group gathered at the *Church of the Holy Spirit, the Shrine Church of the Divine Mercy* in Rome, in May, 1995, in response to the Holy Father's appeal to *"Be Apostles of Divine Mercy."* Pope John Paul II celebrated Mercy Sunday at the church ten days earlier. The retreat, co-directed by Father Glenn Sudano, C.F.R. and Kathleen Keefe included a priest from Nepal and laity from the United States, Malaysia and South Africa.

1995-New York. Bishop Francisco Garmendia of New York was
the main celebrant on Mercy Sunday at the Marian Shrine in West
Haverstraw, N.Y. The first day-long bi-lingual Mercy Sunday celebration drew fourteen hundred people. The event was sponsored
by the Salesians and Peace Through Divine Mercy Apostolate.
The annual celebration began in 1994 when Fr. Allué was Shrine
Rector.

Mary Help of Christians and Mother of the Church guide and protect
us in our work of renewal through the Divine Mercy.

1996-Cracow, Poland. Bishop Emilio Allué, S.D.B., pauses before the miraculous Cracow image of The Divine Mercy enthroned in the Convent chapel. Beneath the altar is the tomb of Blessed Faustina.

1996-Cracow, Poland. A momentous event as Franciszek Cardinal Macharski, Archbishop of Cracow, and protector of the Divine Mercy message and devotion, opens the *First Conference on the Apostolic Movement of Divine Mercy.* Presenters included four Polish Bishops and a member of the Congregation of Sisters. Seventeen countries were represented at the two-day conference held at the Shrine.

1996-Cracow, Poland. Cardinal Macharski welcomes Bishop Allué and Kathleen Keefe to the conference. The Bishops stressed that the Holy Father depends on Divine Mercy to rebuild trust in human beings destroyed by sin. The conference highlighted the gift of *Faustinian Spirituality* to the world.

OUR COMMITMENT
as
APOSTLES OF DIVINE MERCY

In accepting God's Will and the action of the Holy Spirit with open hearts, we begin our journey as *Apostles of Mercy*. This journey will lead many souls touched by the grace and love of a merciful God to become dynamic apostles.

As apostles, we are the messengers of peace and mercy, sharing in the mission given to the Church to evangelize, to heal, and to bring Christ's peace to all we meet. We are committed to a life of prayer for the conversion of sinners and atonement for our sins and the sins of the world.

Our commitment consists in trusting Jesus and practicing mercy by deed, word and prayer. **Peace Through Divine Mercy's** particular emphasis is on:

- the living presence of the Merciful Jesus acting in the Sacraments of Mercy, mainly the **Holy Eucharist** and **Reconciliation (914, 1447, 1602);**

- venerating the **Sacred Image of Divine Mercy;** celebrating the **Feast of Mercy;** praying the **Chaplet of Divine Mercy;** venerating God's Mercy at the 3 o'clock **Hour of Mercy,** according to the requests of Our Lord; **spreading devotion** to the Divine Mercy (341, 300, 476, 1572, 1521);

- **Enthroning the Image of the Divine Mercy in homes and churches and consecrating the Family to the Merciful Jesus,** who effects renewal in the family (570, 441);

- **Total Consecration to Jesus through Mary;** prayerfully meditating on the mysteries of the **Holy Rosary;** investiture in the **Brown Scapular of Our Lady of Mount Carmel;** daily reading from **Scripture;**

- **Praying and sacrificing daily for the priests** of the world (41, 531, 1155);

- Performing the **Corporal and Spiritual Works of Mercy** as a sacrificial offering as victims of Divine Love for mankind (742, 1316).

Works of Mercy

Corporal	Spiritual
1. Feed the hungry	1. Admonish sinners
2. Give drink to the thirsty	2. Instruct the uninformed
3. Clothe the naked	3. Counsel the doubtful
4. Shelter the homeless	4. Comfort the sorrowful
5. Comfort the imprisoned	5. Be patient with those in error
6. Visit the sick	6. Forgive offenses
7. Bury the dead	7. Pray for the living and the dead

Daily attendance at Mass and reception of the Holy Eucharist for those who are in a position to receive Our Lord is the ideal. Frequent reception of the Sacrament of Penance is also an important part of maintaining a close, personal relationship with Jesus. While it is understandable that many are not in a position to attend Mass daily, or may not be able to receive the sacraments, there is still an obligation to attend Mass on Sundays and holy days of obligation. We encourage each person to pray for the resolution of any situation which blocks full participation in the life of the Church.

Chapter 4

PRIESTLY RENEWAL

"To priests who proclaim and extol My mercy, I will give wondrous power; I will anoint their words and touch the hearts of those to whom they will speak" (Diary 1521).

Prayer of Sister Faustina
for Priests

O my Jesus, I beg You on behalf of the whole Church: Grant it love and the light of Your Spirit, and give power to the words of priests so that hardened hearts might be brought to repentance and return to You, O Lord. Lord, give us holy priests; You yourself maintain them in holiness. O Divine and Great High Priest, may the power of Your mercy accompany them everywhere and protect them from the devil's traps and snares which are continually being set for the souls of priests. May the power of Your mercy, O Lord, shatter and bring to naught all that might tarnish the sanctity of priests, for You can do all things. (1052)

Priestly Renewal

"I desire that priests proclaim this great mercy of Mine towards souls of sinners" (Diary 50).

Peace Through Divine Mercy's work of priestly renewal includes our commitment to pray and sacrifice for priests; to promote the message of Divine Mercy among priests; to encourage and support the mission of **Priests of the Enthronement** to enthrone Jesus, King of Mercy in every home and church; to work in parishes with priests to establish the devotion to the Divine Mercy; and to conduct *Divine Mercy Priests' Retreats* based on the model established in Italy.

The Priests' Retreat Ministry was founded by Fr. Joseph Pius Martin, O.F.M.,Cap. and Kathleen Keefe in San Giovanni Rotondo, Italy on the eve of the beatification of Sister Faustina in 1993. Fr. Joseph foresees the retreats as an outgrowth of the ministry of Padre Pio extended to the priests of the world. The first retreat for English speaking priests was held in Italy in July 1994 in the shadow of the Priest-Victim, Padre Pio. The first Spanish language retreat was held in Honduras in October 1995.

The theme of the retreats is "Heal the Shepherd - Heal the Flock" and centers on the renewal of priesthood, considering the priest as pilgrim, penitent and partner with Christ. Although the foundation of the retreat ministry is in San Giovanni Rotondo, where Padre Pio lived out his Victim-Priesthood, we anticipate the retreats being held in many different parts of the world, with the spirit of Padre Pio and his life as Victim-Priest key to the retreats. Padre Pio was a living vessel of mercy and as such is a modern day role model for the priest who seeks renewal. His life exemplified the message of Divine Mercy.

The following excerpt is taken from Kathleen's reflections after the first retreat was held. It gives a flavor of the spirit of the retreat ministry. The complete article appeared in *The Voice of Padre Pio*, Vol. XXIV, No. 12, 1994.

The First Priests' Retreat

The Scripture readings on July 17th of this year had special significance to a group of American priests attending the first *"Divine Mercy Priests' Retreat"* in Italy. Traveling to the peaceful setting of San Giovanni Rotondo on the Gargano Mountain, they experienced the power of the Word of God to heal hearts and renew spirits.

As co-director of the retreat, I share my reflections from the very privileged vantage point of a laywoman called to establish a retreat ministry to priests during a period of the extraordinary outpouring of divine mercy. The prophetic aspect of this ministry is very much in keeping with the prophetic task Jesus has given the Church in its mission to preach and teach the Gospel. Padre Pio's life exemplifies the call of the Master to proclaim the Good News in this apocalyptic age. What better place to begin our journey.

Priest as Pilgrim

Why go to San Giovanni Rotondo on retreat? It is precisely the role of pilgrim that brings one in touch with the reality that we are a pilgrim people on a journey to eternal life. Freely, we choose to leave behind home, family and those dear to us. Security and comfort become vague memories. Crossing the Atlantic, sacrificing sleep and perhaps vacation time, we embrace fatigue and inconvenience, language barriers and strangers, who become appointed companions on the journey. Like dependent children, we rely on our Father to direct and renew us in a manner known only to Him.

Journeying to San Giovanni Rotondo as a pilgrim restores one's sense of the sacred. Leaving behind the world of our experience, we focus on the supernatural revealed in and through the life of Padre Pio. In a setting ordained by the Master Planner we spend one afternoon at Monte Sant' Angelo to honor the great St. Michael the Archangel, who graced this region with his appearance some 1500 years before.

A blessed time of a call to sacrifice everything, we pray: *Lord, I come that I might be healed and renewed. Imbue in me the spirit of Padre Pio, your victim-priest who willingly embraced the Cross, wearing your wounds before the world as a "living crucifix."*

It is pure gift offered by God to his priests!

Priest as Penitent

The first recorded statement of Jesus' public ministry was: **"The kingdom of heaven is at hand. Repent and believe the good news"** - Mk. 1:15. It is in repenting of our sins that we reject evil and embrace God. Without true repentance, there can be no healing. It is a contrite heart that is healed. The psalmist says: **"My sacrifice is a humble spirit, O God; You will not reject a humble and contrite heart"** - Ps 51:17.

It is in the silence of retreat from the world that we are free to open ourselves to the grace to experience revulsion at having offended God. In this experience is that encounter with divine mercy which Jesus expressed to Blessed Faustina: *"Every time you go to confession, immerse yourself entirely in My mercy with great trust, so that I may pour the bounty of My grace upon your soul. When you approach the confessional, know this, that I Myself am waiting there for you. I am only hidden by the priest, but I Myself act in your soul. Here the misery of the soul meets the God of mercy"* (1602).

The priest as penitent encounters Christ in the model of the humble friar whose zeal for souls was so great that he asked God *"to pour out on me the punishments prepared for sinners and for the souls in a state of purgation, even increasing them a hundredfold..."(Letters 1).* But it is the priest as penitent encountering Christ in the confessional, through the ministry of his brother priest, that draws him into that deeper conversion that convicts his spirit anew that it truly is Christ waiting there for him.

At San Giovanni Rotondo the priest is graced to witness the sign of conversion in the endless lines of repentant sinners He can now look at empty confessionals and know that it is not a reflection of the ineffectiveness of the priesthood but rather man's loss of the sense of sin and his failure to see through spiritual eyes the healing power in this great sacrament of mercy.

The humble friar continues to call lost sheep to the fold through the Sacrament of Reconciliation as well as be present to his brother priests to remind them of their need to be healed through repentance. This encounter with mercy empowers the priest to call back the lost sheep to the fold. Healing the flock is the natural outgrowth of the priest penitent who has been healed.

Priest as Partner with Christ

The priest as partner with Christ has the unique privilege of calling down on the altar Christ the Victim who offers himself to the Father in the mystery of the Mass. As partner, the priest shares in the very essence of Christ's life and mission. Renewal of the priest heightens our awareness of Christ's presence in the person of the priest, and releases the fullness of the Spirit of Christ in our midst. This outpouring of divine mercy through the priest is manifested in power through teaching, preaching, healing, miracles and the compassionate love and mercy that pour out of the priest who is truly a partner with Christ. Like Jesus, the priest who is healed and renewed **"calls his own sheep by name, and he leads them out. When he has brought them out, he goes ahead of them, and the sheep follow him because they know his voice"** - Jn 10:3-4.

This partnership is reflected in the mysterious brotherhood that exists when priests are drawn together in the worship of God, the sharing of the joy of ministering to one another, the grace of confessing to each other, the fellowship of love lived out for a higher purpose - that of total surrender to the martyrdom that comes from being the ultimate sign of contradiction in the world.

This was Padre Pio's gift to God and to his fellow man. This model of unconditional love is the mysterious gift offered to priests today when they respond to Jesus' invitation: **"Let us go off by ourselves to some place where we will be alone and you can rest a while"** - Mk. 6:31.

Priests of the Enthronement

Priests of the Enthronement is one of the apostolic works of *Peace Through Divine Mercy* which fulfills our mission of priestly renewal. Our Lord is reaching out to His priests in these merciless times, asking them to proclaim His mercy. He promises to give them *"wondrous power,"* to touch hearts (1521). **Priests of the Enthronement** are being raised up as living witnesses to the power of the holy priesthood and the truth of Jesus' words.

Priests of the Enthronement experience a new fire within - a renewing of their spirits as they reach out to touch souls with the mercy of God. It is in the selfless pouring out of themselves like "streams of living water" that souls are renewed and transformed. The priest in union with the Merciful Jesus has a special power to heal wounded and broken souls as he continually drinks from the wellspring of God's love. *"I have opened My heart as a living fountain of mercy. Let all souls draw life from it,"* Jesus said (1520).

Priests of the Enthronement respond to the requests of Jesus made through His servant, Blessed Faustina: to glorify and proclaim God's mercy (570); administer healing to the body, mind and spirit through the Sacraments of Mercy (206); give every soul access to it [the image](570), which is done by *Enthronement of the Image of the Divine Mercy*, thus drawing humanity back into the mystery of their salvation.

Chapter 5

FAMILY RENEWAL

"Behold, the treasures of grace that flow down upon souls, but not all souls know how to take advantage of My generosity" (Diary 1687).

St. Joseph

St. Joseph, Guardian of the Holy Family, intercede for all families to be renewed and united in the love of the Merciful Jesus.

Prayer For Families

Grant that love, strengthened by the grace of the Sacrament of Marriage, may prove mightier than all the weaknesses and trials through which our families pass. Through the intercession of the Holy Family of Nazareth, grant that the Church may fruitfully carry out her worldwide mission in the family and through the family. Through Christ Our Lord who is the Way, the Truth and the Life for ever and ever. Amen.

John Paul II

FAMILY RENEWAL

Peace Through Divine Mercy is committed to the renewal of the family through *Enthronement of the Image of the Divine Mercy* and the spread of devotion to the Divine Mercy in all its aspects.

In God's perfect wisdom, He created the model for all families. We look to that model which gave the world its Savior and Redeemer - the Holy Family. Almighty God sent His Son to live as a child and to grow into manhood in obedience to the Father, through the perfect obedience of the members of the Holy Family.

This is a vital concept to embrace at a time when we are often frustrated and perplexed by the world's definition of what constitutes a happy family. Every mother and father, every single parent or guardian, struggling to raise a family in the most difficult of times, has a heavenly Father and Mother to guide them. This is the unity found only in the Body of Christ and it is always complete and perfect when it is in the Blessed Trinity, Father, Son and Holy Spirit.

This means that we must not accept the world's definition of "family," but rather, embrace God's model of family and live in its spirit of humility and obedience. A loving God surely desires the restoration of the family, but it can only be restored by man's obedience to God, in the life he or she is called to and within the context of the sacredness of marriage and procreation. God has created an ordered universe and calls man to restore order to his life. When each of us recognizes this call to an ordered life, a life of obedience to God, the grace of God will flow into our lives, into our families, our relationships and friendships, into our society and our world.

Today, more than ever before, we are in desperate need of the mercy of God to restore man's dignity as a child of God.

Mary's Role

Mary ever remains a symbol of God's love for us. She is our humble and loving Mother whose protective mantle shields us from the forces of evil and guides us back to her Son. It is Mary, in her role as Mother, who is the guiding force in restoring man's understanding of the sacredness of human life and the privileged role that women play in the family and in the society. Mary is a unifying presence in the family. She affirms the mother as the very heart (life) of the family and the father as protector and head of the family.

To understand Mary's role in the family, one must accept her as the model of motherhood. In this capacity, Mary forms the woman in her role as mother, helping the woman to understand and accept the dignity and sacredness of her role in God's plan of creation. Pope John Paul II addressed this question of dignity when he said:

The dignity of every human being and the vocation corresponding to that dignity find their definitive measure in union with God. Mary, the woman of the Bible, is the most complete expression of this dignity and vocation. For no human being, male or female, created in the image and likeness of God, can in any way attain fulfillment apart from this image and likeness. (*On the Dignity and Vocation of Women*, 5)

Family Renewal Comes Through
the Merciful Heart of Jesus

"My mercy has passed into souls through the divine-human heart of Jesus as a ray from the sun passes through crystal" (528).

The beautiful parable of "The Vine and the Branches" speaks to us of all we can be in Christ. In a world of broken dreams, broken hearts and broken lives, we must turn to the

Merciful Jesus who has promised to heal aching mankind. He alone is the source of our peace.

The Vine and the Branches

"Live on in me, as I do in you.
No more than a branch can bear fruit of itself
Apart from the vine,
can you bear fruit, apart from me.
I am the vine, you are the branches,
He who lives in me and I in him,
will produce abundantly,
for apart from me you can do nothing.
A man who does not live in me is like a
   withered, rejected branch,
picked up to be thrown in the fire and burnt.
If you live in me, and my words stay part of you,
you may ask what you will-
it will be done for you" - John 15:4-7.

When we are united in Christ, our strength is drawn daily from the vine. Clearly and intimately, we are told that who we are is in relation to the Source of Life and that as long as we remain in that relationship, we will bear much fruit; but if we do not, we are as a branch that has been broken from the vine, falling to earth, rejected and withered, unable to bear fruit.

Christ has given us a clear and concise description of how to achieve our fullest potential as children of God. We must live in Him and He must live in us. This union of creature and Creator is a reciprocal one, alive and ongoing. Man must receive the Lord into His life and seek to live in the Lord. Jesus asks us to enter freely into His Merciful Heart and we will produce abundantly.

A loving mother who nurtures her child, knows the heart of the child. She knows the needs of the child before the child ever asks. She knows what is good for the child, and what is not good. When both the mother and child fulfill their roles, the child also knows what is and what is not good for him. How often have our mothers and fathers or our loved ones anticipated our needs simply because their spirits were in union with our spirits and their love motivated them to act. This key point explains why there is no peace in the lives of young people who live in homes where the spiritual bond has been broken; why there is no peace between husband and wife who are not in union with God.

Is this not what Jesus is saying to us? We are made in His image and likeness; no one knows the creature like the Creator.

> **"Can a mother forget her infant,**
> **be without tenderness for the child of her womb?**
> **Even should she forget,**
> **I will never forget you.**
> **See, upon the palms of my hands**
> **I have written your name;**
> **your walls are ever before me"** - Isaiah 49:15-16.

This is the gift that Jesus offers us. He will never forget us. He has written our name on the palms of His hands; this is His love poured out - His Divine Mercy. It is through His mercy that our lives and our families will be healed and restored. However, we cannot postpone that day of conversion. It is *now* that the graces of conversion and healing are offered to humanity. *This is the day of Divine Mercy.* May He be enthroned in every heart and in every home; may He be praised and adored throughout the world; and may His words to Sister Faustina be ever on our lips: *Jesus, I trust in You.*

Family Renewal Ministry

In order to accomplish family renewal, the apostolate offers lay retreats and days of recollection in parishes and retreat houses as well as parish missions.

The lay retreat ministry was founded in San Giovanni Rotondo, Italy in 1995. It is an in-depth experience for *Apostles of Divine Mercy* who wish to become more involved in the apostolate's work of upholding the ministerial priesthood and working for the renewal of families through the Divine Mercy. The retreat experience is the basis for growth in the spirituality of the Apostles, and for their total consecration to Jesus through Mary. These retreats are scheduled throughout the United States and in other countries.

The Gift of New Life

A Family Prayer for Renewal

Lord God, we thank You and praise Your goodness for the gift of life You have given us. We know, Lord, that our children are Your children. You have entrusted them to us for a short time, to nurture them, love them, and send them out as Your disciples to a world that hungers for Your love and peace.

Help us, Lord, to prune them so that they bear fruit that is rich and sweet. Help us through the seasons of their young lives and the seasons of our advancing years, to shed the trappings of this world, just as Your trees shed their leaves to face winter's onslaught.

Help us to stand barren and naked before You in the winter of our dying. Veil us in humility so that we may see You in all of creation, despite the clouds of darkness that envelop Your world; hear You in the winds of change that blow across Your universe; feel You in our hearts that long to die to the selfishness of our natures.

Bring us all to new life in You; to the flowering of virtue within us; to the sunshine of Your love and peace. For it is in dying, You destroyed our death, rising, You restored our life. Lord, Jesus, come in glory.

Kathleen Keefe ©1988

Chapter 6

ENTHRONEMENT
of
the
IMAGE
of
THE DIVINE MERCY
in
THE HOME

<u>Enthronement of the Image of the Divine Mercy is</u>:

A Moment of Grace
when Jesus comes to our homes,
imperfect as they may be,
to establish His Kingdom of Love and Redemption.

<u>Enthronement of the Image of the Divine Mercy is</u>:

An Experience of Jesus' Love
realized in time and space, coming toward souls
to transform them, to heal them and to renew them.

<u>Enthronement of the Image of the Divine Mercy is</u>:

A Gift of God
to instill Hope and Trust
in a world mentality of despair, superficiality and unbelief.

<u>Enthronement of the Image of the Divine Mercy is</u>:

A Means to Counteract
the secularist influence
and restore family ties and Christian values
through the practice of mercy by deed, word and prayer.

<u>Enthronement of the Image of the Divine Mercy is</u>:

A Tool of Evangelization
as the Merciful Jesus comes
to bring each member His gospel, His teaching, His very life.
It instructs the mind and moves the heart to action.

INTRODUCTION

Today, more than ever before, our families, society and the world need the loving presence of a forgiving God. Unrest, violence and immorality must be countered with divine grace. Jesus came to bring redemption and peace to broken mankind; that true peace must begin within the basic unit of society, the family.

Enthronement of the Image of the Divine Mercy in the home provides the opportunity for evangelization and building the faith of its members. The Merciful Jesus meets the family at the level of faith proper to each member. A welcoming attitude of humility and belief allows Jesus to work miracles of grace in souls.

Enthronement provides a *special* welcome for Jesus to come into our hearts and homes to claim them for Himself. He alone is the Way, the Truth and the Life. When the grace of God reigns in the members of a family, the presence of the Holy Spirit increases the divine life in them, immersing them in the sacraments of His mercy.

The Lord, who is aware of our sinfulness and our struggles with the prince of darkness, reaches out with His mercy to heal and forgive. On one occasion, Jesus accepted the invitation to dine in the home of Zacchaeus, the chief tax collector and a wealthy man, who, in the opinion of the people, was a sinner. However, after hearing his profession of good deeds, Jesus declared: **"Salvation has come to this house today"** -Luke 19:9-10. In like manner, by enthroning the Merciful Jesus in our homes, we are responding to Jesus' wish: **"I must stay in your house today"** -Luke 19:5.

Enthronement of the Image of the Divine Mercy is needed today with an urgency proper to prophetic times. Bleak as the family situation may appear, the mercy of God instills hope and trust. The Image of the Divine Mercy in the home presents the love of a caring Father, the mercy of the Redeeming Son, and the sanctifying grace of the Holy Spirit. The rays descend and penetrate into the interior life of a soul snatching it from the grasp of the devil.

Families who have experienced conversions and healings through *Enthronement of the Image of the Divine Mercy* in their homes are among the best evangelizers. When faith has been renewed and strengthened, marriages have been restored, children have been healed, souls have been led back to the embrace of the Merciful Jesus through the work of enthronement, can we doubt that Jesus is showing us the path to healing and restoration.

Veneration of the image painted according to the pattern requested by Jesus Himself, offers an oasis of joy, forgiveness, confidence and trust in our world today. The Creator, Father rich in mercy, continues to offer mankind His everlasting love, and His enduring merciful forgiveness.

As you begin reading the *Enthronement of the Image of the Divine Mercy and the Nine Graces of Enthronement in the Home,* we ask that you prayerfully enter into the mystery of God's mercy, imploring the Holy Spirit to enlighten your mind and fill your heart with the desire to be an apostle of God's mercy in the family, the community and the world. Read the material slowly and often. Meditate on the richness of God's blessings as revealed in His Word and through the private revelations of Blessed Faustina.

Blessed Sr. Faustina Kowalska
and
The Image of the Divine Mercy

*"Not in the beauty of the color, nor of the brush lies
the greatness of this image, but in My grace"* (Diary, 313).

On February 22, 1931 Our Lord appeared in a vision to a humble, young Polish nun, Sister Faustina Kowalska. Jesus chose Sr. Faustina to be the Apostle and "Secretary of His Divine Mercy" to the contemporary world. The depth of her spirituality and the extraordinary graces bestowed upon her by Jesus are revealed in her Diary published in 1981. She was particularly graced to enter into the mystery of Divine Mercy in order to share it with mankind in these critical times that cry out for God's mercy. The specific forms of the devotion to the Divine Mercy as revealed to Sister Faustina are incorporated into the work of the *Enthronement of the Image of the Divine Mercy* in the home.

Sister Faustina received the express mandate from Our Lord to *"Paint an image according to the pattern you see, with the signature: 'Jesus, I trust in you.' I desire that this image be venerated, first in your chapel, and then throughout the world"* (47). The first painting of the Divine Mercy was completed in June 1934 by Eugene Kazimierowski. Subsequently, many other versions have been rendered by artists. However, the painting by Adolf Hyla, which hangs over the tomb of Blessed Faustina at the Shrine of Divine Mercy in Lagiewniki, Cracow, Poland remains the most popular version throughout the world.

Adolf Hyla's original painting was a votive offering in thanksgiving for his family's safety and survival during the war. It was blessed on May 7, 1943. A smaller canvas was completed by Hyla to fit into the space over the side altar where it was set up permanently. Fr. Jozef Andrasz, S.J., Sister Faustina's second spiritual director, blessed the image on April 16, 1944 on the occasion of the first solemn celebration in honor of the Divine

Mercy in the convent chapel. In 1954 Adolf Hyla painted a dark background over the original one and put a tiled floor under the feet of Jesus. This representation, although not the original painting, has gained a reputation as a source of innumerable graces.

The Image of the Divine Mercy
a prayerful poem

"O Eternal Love, You command Your Sacred Image to
be painted
And reveal to us the inconceivable fount of mercy,
You bless whoever approaches Your rays,
And a soul all black will turn into snow.

O sweet Jesus, it is here You established the throne of
Your mercy
To bring joy and hope to sinful man.
From Your open Heart, as from a pure fount,
Flows comfort to a repentant heart and soul.

May praise and glory for this image
Never cease to stream from man's soul.
May praise of God's mercy pour from every heart,
Now, and at every hour, and forever and ever" (Diary, 1).

by

Sister M. Faustina Kowalska
Apostle and Secretary of Divine Mercy

Chapter 7

NINE GRACES OF ENTHRONEMENT OF THE IMAGE OF THE DIVINE MERCY IN THE HOME

"Every soul in its relation to Me will contemplate My love and mercy throughout eternity" (Diary, 699).

The Divine Mercy devotion, a gift from God specific to the times we live in, involves each of us in both a contemplative and active apostolate of love and mercy, faith and trust, atonement, intercession and evangelization. *"I claim veneration for My mercy from every creature,"* Jesus said (1572). Our response is enthronement, an act of love and trust to praise and thank Jesus. His Kingship is proclaimed by placing the image in a prominent place in the home and consecrating the family to His mercy. Our humble and committed participation leads to a vibrant interaction with Our Savior who offers us the graces of conversion and healing.

In faith, we begin our journey in the footsteps of Jesus who raised up this devotion to His Mercy for these times, calling it *"...the last hope of salvation"* (998).

Diary of Sr. Faustina M. Kowalska, Divine Mercy in my Soul, copyright © 1987 Congregation of Marians of the Immaculate Conception; all world rights reserved; printed with permission.

Diary entry numbers are printed after each quotation.

I. Enthronement of the Image of the Divine Mercy is an act of love and trust in the Merciful Jesus, who enters our home and becomes part of our family.

"Proclaim that mercy is the greatest attribute of God. All the works of my hands are crowned with mercy" (Diary, 301).

Enthronement is a first step in responding to the gift of Divine Mercy. Jesus is welcomed into the home and invited to be part of the family. In opening our homes to the King of Mercy, we open our hearts to the action of grace. *"My mercy works in all those hearts which open their doors to it,"* Jesus said to Sister Faustina (1577). The home becomes the place of encounter with Jesus who wishes to walk with us on our earthly pilgrimage.

Jesus dignified every dwelling He entered by His mere presence, beginning with a stable in Bethlehem which He chose as His birthplace. His life in Nazareth, where He grew and lived in obedience to Mary and Joseph for thirty of His thirty-three years, demonstrates the great value He placed on the sacredness of the home and the family. Every home, every dwelling place, however inadequate in the eyes of man, becomes a throne room for the King of Mercy when He is invited to dwell in it and sanctify it by His presence.

We invite you now to enter into the grace of this moment. This is Jesus, Lord and Savior whose Mercy brings Him to your home to become part of your family. Welcome Him with love and trust, in total expectation of the transforming action of His Holy Spirit in your life and in your family. Your spirit of love and trust prepare you for the limitless graces Jesus offers to you through His Divine and Merciful Heart.

II. Enthronement of the Image of the Divine Mercy is an act of praise and thanksgiving for God's Mercy. It raises the soul to a higher degree of conversion and grace.

"In the Old Covenant I sent prophets wielding thunderbolts to My people. Today I am sending you with My mercy to the people of the whole world. I do not want to punish aching mankind, but I desire to heal it, pressing it to My Merciful Heart. I use punishment when they themselves force Me to do so; My hand is reluctant to take hold of the sword of justice. Before the Day of Justice I am sending the Day of Mercy" (Diary, 1588).

Throughout the history of salvation God has demonstrated His power, His dominion, His forgiveness through signs, wonders and visible miracles. The Old Testament is full of these outward manifestations of His mercy. In the fullness of time, He sent His Son, made flesh for our salvation. It is through Jesus, the Mediator, that we reach the Father and the Father shares His divine life with us. Jesus expressed this to His disciples when He said: **"He who sees me, see the Father,"**-John.14:9 and **"I am the Way, the Truth and the Life"** -John 14:6.

Being the revelation of the Father and the second Person of the Trinity, Jesus becomes our intercessor and the incarnation of God's merciful love. Jesus is Mercy itself. Consequently, His image evokes in the soul the presence of Him who comes to save, to heal, to forgive, to communicate the life of the Father. The image of Divine Mercy is God's gift to mankind in these times to lift the soul to a higher degree of conversion and of grace. *"Already there are many souls who have been drawn to My love by this image,"* Jesus said. *"My mercy acts in souls through this work"* (1379).

Enthronement of the Image of the Divine Mercy in the home as an act of praise and thanksgiving opens the family to the action of the Holy Spirit. The floodgates of God's mercy open to souls who praise and thank Him in all circumstances. It also serves as a reminder of the urgency to live mercy in the family, pray for mercy on the family and proclaim mercy in the family and the world. The Mother of God spoke to Sister Faustina about this work, encouraging her not to fear and to be faithful to the end. *"I gave the Savior to the world; as for you, you have to speak to the world about His great mercy and prepare the world for the Second Coming of Him who will come, not as a merciful Savior, but as a just Judge. Oh, how terrible is that day!..Determined is the day of justice, the day of divine wrath. The angels tremble before it"* (635).

Sister Faustina willingly accepted the mission and the suffering involved in bringing the message of Divine Mercy to the world. *"It will be a new splendor for the Church..."* she wrote. *"That God is infinitely merciful, no one can deny. He desires everyone to know this before He comes again as Judge. He wants souls to come to know Him first as King of Mercy"* (378).

Enthronement of the Image of the Divine Mercy draws us to the Merciful Heart of Jesus, source of all healing. He comes, in this "Day of Mercy," not to judge us but to pour out His mercy; not to condemn us but to heal our shame; not to burden us but to carry our burdens; not to strip us but to clothe us in righteousness; not to punish us but to forgive our sins; not to bring death but to give us life in the Eucharist. *"Let us take advantage of mercy while there is still time for mercy,"* Sister Faustina advises (1035).

We praise and thank God for His great mercy. *"Be grateful for the smallest of My graces because your gratitude compels Me to grant you new graces"* (1701). We rejoice in His justice which we anticipate with confidence and trust, for scripture says: **"He will completely wipe out the merciless and the arrogant, and will destroy the authority of the wicked. He will give every person what his thoughts and actions deserve. Because of the Lord's mercy, His people will be happy when He has judged their case. In times of trouble His mercy is as welcome as rain after a long drought"** -Sirach 35:18-20.

III. Enthronement of the Image of the Divine Mercy draws us into the Paschal Mysteries as reflected in the image.

" I desire that you know more profoundly the love that burns in My heart for souls, and you will understand this when you meditate upon My Passion" (Diary, 186).

The theological value of this image is determined solely by the Person it represents, Jesus Christ, the High Priest and Mediator between God and man. The image is a visual representation of the Merciful Jesus which helps us to grasp the reality of God's love for us. Through our eyes the mind is inspired to contemplation and the heart moved to action. *"There are few souls who contemplate My Passion with true feeling,"* Jesus said. *"I give great graces to souls who meditate devoutly on My Passion"* (737).

With His left hand, Jesus points to His pierced heart from which *"immediately blood and water flowed out"* -John 19:31-34. The Good Friday event of the Crucifixion is symbolized in the two rays which *"...denote Blood and Water. The pale ray stands for the water which makes souls righteous. The red ray stands for the Blood which is the life of souls...The two rays issued forth from the very depths of My tender mercy when My agonized Heart was opened by a lance on the cross"* (299).

Jesus said: *"My gaze from this image is like My gaze from the cross"* (326). *Enthronement of the Image of the Divine Mercy* opens our souls to the loving gaze of Jesus, in a personal encounter that deepens our awareness of His love for us. It is He who effects in us that change of heart that is key to our transformation. **"I will give them a new heart and a new mind. I will take away their stubborn heart of stone and will give them an obedient heart"** -Ezekiel 11:19.

Desiring to draw us further into the graces and mystery of His Passion and Death, Our Lord instructed Sister Faustina about the manner in which graces could be obtained: *"...as often as you hear the clock strike the third hour, immerse yourself completely in My mercy, adoring and glorifying it; invoke its omnipotence for the whole world, and particularly for poor sinners; for at that moment mercy was opened wide for every soul. In this hour you can obtain everything for yourself and for others for the asking"* (1572).

Our Lord also asked Sister Faustina to make the Stations of the Cross, if possible, at the hour of mercy or to briefly adore Him in the Blessed Sacrament; *"...and should you be unable to step into the chapel, immerse yourself in prayer there where you happen to be, if only for a very brief instant"* (1572). The great emphasis placed on meditating on the Passion is a lesson in the spiritual life given by Jesus Himself.

The theme of the Resurrection is central to the Image of the Divine Mercy. Contemplating the glory of the Son of God who conquered suffering and death, the image portrays the triumphant Jesus, clothed in a white robe, His hand raised in blessing, His eyes full of concern for all humanity. It is the compassionate Son of God reaching out with the grace of conversion through the Sacraments of Mercy. The two rays come down to us inviting our participation in His divine life. He is the resurrected Savior who sends His Spirit and remains forever as the source of grace and life.

IV.   Enthronement of the Image of the Divine Mercy deepens our love and understanding of the Sacraments of Mercy to heal, renew and transform our lives.

"The Feast of Mercy emerged from My very depths of tenderness. It is my desire that it be solemnly celebrated on the first Sunday after Easter. Mankind will not have peace until it turns to the Fount of My Mercy" (Diary, 699).

In designating the first Sunday after Easter as Mercy Sunday (49), Jesus wants us to see the connection to His Resurrection as well as the healing power of the Sacraments of Reconciliation and Holy Eucharist. The role of the priest is paramount in **proclaiming** mercy: *"On that day, priests are to tell everyone about My great and unfathomable mercy"* (570); **administering** healing to the body, mind and spirit; *"...On the day of My Feast...you will go through the whole world and bring fainting souls to the spring of My mercy. I shall heal and strengthen them"* (206); and **blessing** the image for public veneration: *"...I want the image to be solemnly blessed on the first Sunday after Easter, and I want it to be venerated publicly so that every soul may know about it,"* Jesus directed (341).

In the gospel for that day, Jesus gave His apostles the power to forgive sins. In these days, Jesus gives us a renewed appreciation of the healing power of this sacrament through His words to Sister Faustina: *"Tell souls where they are to look for solace; that is, in the Tribunal of Mercy. There the greatest miracles take place and are incessantly repeated...Were a soul like a decaying corpse so that from a human standpoint, there would be no hope of restoration...the miracle of Divine Mercy restores that soul in full"* (1448). Jesus desires that the Feast be *"a refuge and shelter for all souls, and especially for poor sinners"* (699).

The miracle of spiritual healing in the Sacraments of Mercy is confirmed by these words of Jesus: *"The soul that will go to Confession and receive Holy Communion shall obtain complete forgiveness of sins and punishment. On that day all the divine floodgates through which grace flow are opened"* (699). Miracles of spiritual healing often result in physical and emotional healing as well as freedom from bondage.

One illustration of the healing power of the Eucharist occurred when a very ill Sr. Faustina received Holy Communion. She described an interior prompting to pray these particular words: *'Jesus, may Your pure and healthy blood circulate in my ailing organism, and may Your pure and healthy body transform my weak body, and may a healthy and vigorous life throb within me, if it is truly Your holy will...'"* (1089). She experienced an instant physical healing.

Graces are also obtained by praying the chaplet for nine days before the Feast, beginning on Good Friday. *"By this novena,"* Jesus said, *"I will grant every possible grace"* (796).

Enthronement of the Image of the Divine Mercy opens the family to the limitless graces flowing from the Merciful Jesus who promised that *"Every soul believing and trusting in My mercy will obtain it"* (420). Enthronement draws the family to participate in the Feast of Mercy, where their love and understanding of the Sacraments of Mercy to heal, renew and transform lives is deepened, restored or perhaps understood for the first time.

V. Enthronement of the Image of the Divine Mercy brings Christ's Peace to the Home

"Tell aching mankind to snuggle close to My merciful Heart and I will fill it with peace" (Diary, 1074).

The peace of Christ is intimately connected to the Holy Eucharist and Reconciliation. These sacraments of love, peace, healing and forgiveness continue through the ministry of the priest. Jesus' peace penetrates the soul in confession. *"...I Myself am waiting there for you,"* He said. *"I am only hidden by the priest, but I Myself act in your soul"* (1602). This personal encounter with Jesus in the Sacrament of Reconciliation is key to peace in the soul of the penitent and ultimately, peace in the family through God's radiating graces. **"You, Lord, give perfect peace to those who keep their purpose firm and put their trust in you"** -Isaiah 26:3.

Christ's peace rests in our hearts when we obey His Word and surrender our lives to His Divine Will. *"I am experiencing a profound peace,"* wrote Sr. Faustina, *"and this peace flows from the witness of my conscience, that is to say, that I am always doing Your will, O Lord"* (1326).

In the daily struggles of life, it is easy to lose our focus on the Lord. Briefly pausing to reflect on what Christ has done for us or just stopping to gaze upon the image of the One who carries our burdens and brings us His peace restores our focus as we pray, *"Jesus, I trust in You."*

The home, which is a sanctuary where Christ's peace should dwell, is often the battleground where the forces of evil carry out the systematic destruction of the family. At the root of much of the division in families today is unforgiveness. The farther away we are from a personal relationship with Jesus, the greater will be our unforgiveness towards ourselves and others.

This is reflected in the hostility, resentment and bitterness that often exist among family members; the stubborn refusal to attempt reconciliation; and an attitude of indifference towards those in our family who are in need of love and mercy. This spirit of unforgiveness is in direct opposition to the teachings of Christ. In Matthew's gospel we read: **"...If you are about to offer your gift to God at the altar and there you remember that your brother has something against you, leave your gift here in front of the altar, go at once and make peace with your brother, and then come back and offer your gift to God"** -Matt.5:23-24. The refusal to make peace is frequently traced to the failure to avail ourselves of the graces contained in the Sacrament of Reconciliation. *"Pray for souls that they be not afraid to approach the tribunal of My mercy,"* Jesus said (975). When we do not seek God's forgiveness, we are vulnerable to the spirit of the world which is opposed to the mercy and forgiveness of God.

Enthronement of the Image of the Divine Mercy welcomes Jesus who comes with peace and reconciliation to our family. It introduces the family to the devotion He gave us to heal our brokenness and restore our relationship with Him. Jesus wants us to live and spread the message of mercy and bring His peace to those who share our life and our home; those who are closest to us as well as those who may be the most difficult to love. In the Sermon on the Mount, Jesus said: **"Happy are those who work for peace; God will call them His children!"** -Matt. 5:9. This peace which Christ speaks of is the peace that makes us one with Him; it is the peace that enables us to endure the crosses of life, particularly within our own family; it is the peace that comes through forgiveness. We may not see the effects of peace in our home immediately, but we have the promise contained in scripture that *"...Goodness is the harvest that is produced from the seeds the peacemakers plant in peace"* -Jas. 4:18. Embracing His mercy is our only hope. *"Mankind will not have peace until it turns with trust to My mercy"* (300).

In the face of continued spiritual danger and desolation, we must respond to His command to live and spread the message of mercy, so that all people may experience the peace of Christ in their hearts and in their homes.

VI. Enthronement of the Image of the Divine Mercy strengthens our faith, deepens our trust and increases our love of God.

"The graces of My mercy are drawn by means of one vessel only, and that is-trust. The more a soul trusts the more it will receive" (Diary, 1578).

The spirit of trust is the very essence of the devotion to the Divine Mercy. Trust is the fruit of a humble, contrite heart that has faith in God. The virtue of faith is the foundation of trust. *"...For me to be able to act upon a soul, the soul must have faith,"* (1420) Jesus said to Sister Faustina. Faith helps us to understand God's mercy; understanding His mercy increases our hope and deepens our trust in God. **"In union with Christ and through our faith in Him,"** St. Paul writes, **"we have the boldness to go into God's presence with all confidence"** -Eph. 3:12.

Enthronement of the Image of the Divine Mercy nurtures the precious gift of faith as we seek opportunities to grow in faith, humility and love of God. *"The soul's true greatness,"* Our Lady instructed Sister Faustina, *"is in loving God and in humbling oneself in His presence, completely forgetting oneself...the Lord...is well-pleased only with the humble; He always opposes the proud"* (1711). This insight into the interior life helps us to understand that for a soul to trust, it must be supported by the virtue of humility. *"A humble soul does not trust itself, but places all its confidence in God,"* wrote Sister Faustina (593). Such a soul, conscious of its own sinfulness, is led by grace to the fount of mercy to be healed and educated (377). Healing and self-knowledge draw the soul more deeply into the loving Heart of Jesus, where it is strengthened and transformed into a living channel of mercy. *"An ardent love of God sees all around itself constant opportunities to share itself through deed, word and prayer"* (1313).

We may ask what is to become of family members, friends and neighbors who are weak in faith, indifferent or have completely turned away from God. *"...Your duty is...to beg for this grace for them, so that they too may glorify My mercy,"* Jesus said to Sister Faustina (1160). The merciful Savior reaches out to souls through our prayers and sacrifices. *"There is but one price at which souls are bought, and that is suffering united to My suffering on the cross"* (324). God uses these acts of mercy to restore sinners to life in Christ. *"Conversion, as well as perseverance, is a grace of My mercy,"* Jesus said (1577). *"When you say this prayer, with a contrite heart and with faith on behalf of some sinner, I will give him the grace of conversion. This is the prayer:* (186) *"O Blood and Water, which gushed forth from the Heart of Jesus as a fount of Mercy for us, I trust in You"* (187).

God alone knows our hearts and the inner recesses of our minds. He alone has the power to restore and strengthen what has been lost. He alone is the giver of all gifts. He asks only that we turn to Him in trust and He will answer our prayers.

VII. Enthronement of the Image of the Divine Mercy transforms us into Apostles of Mercy in our families and in the world.

"I am Love and Mercy itself. When a soul approaches Me with trust, I fill it with such an abundance of graces that it cannot contain them within itself, but radiates them to other souls" (Diary, 1074).

In cooperating with the graces unfolding from *Enthronement of the Image of the Divine Mercy,* we experience an increase in faith, hope and charity. The fruit of these virtues is mercy. *"Pure love is the guide of my life, and externally, it is mercy which is its fruit,"* wrote Sister Faustina (1363).

Embracing mercy is not an option but a clear mandate from God expressed in these words to Sr. Faustina: *"If a soul does not exercise mercy somehow or other, it will not obtain My mercy on the day of judgment..."* (1317). *"I am giving you three ways of exercising mercy toward your neighbor: the first-by deed, the second-by word, the third-by prayer. In these three degrees are contained the fullness of mercy and it is an unquestionable proof of love for Me"* (742).

Although there is a logical progression in the soul's journey toward becoming an *Apostle of Mercy,* we must also allow the Holy Spirit the freedom to work miracles of transformation in each of us according to God's Will. Scripture and history are replete with examples of dramatic conversions that defy explanation, most notably, St. Paul, who wrote: **"...God was merciful to me because I did not yet have faith and so did not know what I was doing. Our Lord poured out His abundant grace on me and gave me the faith and love which are ours in union with Christ Jesus"**-1Tim. 1:13-14. Our own misery must never become a stumbling block to our transformation. *"There is no misery that could be a match for My mercy,"* Jesus said, *"neither will misery exhaust it, because as it is being granted-it increases..."* (1273). Clearly, this is God's work - not ours. It is He who transforms us into *Apostles of Mercy. "If souls would put themselves completely in My care,"* Jesus said, *"I Myself would undertake the task of sanctifying them, and I would lavish even greater graces on them"* (1682).

Supported by the promises of the Lord, and fortified by prayer and a sincere desire to be merciful, our role is to begin the practice of mercy within our family. Jesus wants mercy lived out in the ordinary circumstances of daily life. His presence in our home, through the act of enthronement, makes us more aware of the little miracles of grace taking place in our family; miracles we may have previously overlooked. As we venerate the Image of the Divine Mercy, our trust and love increase and we radiate God's grace to others in our family and our community. This grace acts like a magnet drawing souls to the Divine Mercy. *"From this fountain spring all graces for souls"* (1190).

The universality of Jesus' salvation is reflected in His command to have the image venerated *"...throughout the world* (47). *"...If sinners knew My mercy, they would not perish in such great numbers"* (1396).

Enthronement of the Image of the Divine Mercy is a crucial step in restoring the foundation of society - the family. As the family is restored, *Apostles of Mercy* are being formed to spread this worldwide work of evangelization, so that Jesus may dwell in all hearts, all families, and all homes. Through the image, which is the textbook of the theology of the Divine Mercy, we have *"a vessel"* with which *"to keep coming for graces to the fountain of mercy.* That vessel is this image with the signature: *'Jesus, I trust in You'"*(327).

**VIII. Enthronement of the Image of the Divine Mercy leads
us to a deeper life of intercessory prayer
for our families and for the whole world.**

---

*"Oh, what great graces I will grant to souls who say this chaplet; the
very depths of My tender mercy are stirred for the sake of those who
say the chaplet...Speak to the world about My mercy...It is a sign for
the end times; after it will come the day of justice"* (Diary, 848).

Jesus has given us the means to effect miracles in our families and
in the world through our trust and willingness to embrace the Divine
Mercy. One means is the Chaplet of the Divine Mercy in which we unite
our prayer to Jesus' sacrifice on the cross, imploring mercy on ourselves
"and on the whole world."

The prayer was dictated to Sister Faustina in 1935 when she had
a vision of an angel coming to strike a particular place on earth.
Realizing God's anger, she begged the angel not to strike the earth until
the world did penance. She then saw the Holy Trinity. Awestruck, she
could not bring herself to repeat the request for a reprieve. She then
prayed the words which she heard interiorly and the angel was not able to
execute the sentence that had been meted out to the earth for sins
committed against God. Such is the power of the Chaplet of the Divine
Mercy in appeasing God's just anger (474).

Reciting the chaplet is an act of mercy and a powerful prayer of
intercession. *"It pleases Me to grant [souls] everything they ask of Me
when they say the chaplet"* (1541). Sinners enjoy special privileges of
conversion and the forgiveness of sins if they recite the chaplet at the hour
of death in a spirit of trust and repentance or if it said at the bedside of a
dying person (811). Jesus said: *"The prayer most pleasing to Me is
prayer for the conversion of sinners. Know ... that this prayer is
always heard and answered"* (1397).

Intercessory prayer is not limited to the chaplet; rather, the
chaplet should be seen in the context of the Holy Sacrifice of the Mass
and the Mysteries of Christ's life as prayed in the Rosary and reflected in

the Word of God. By intercession we cooperate with Jesus in the work of saving souls. As such, it requires perseverance and sacrifice. Our Lord asked Sister Faustina to be faithful to prayer despite suffering, *"...because oftentimes the realization of God's great plans depends mainly on such prayer, we frustrate what the Lord wanted to do through us or within us"* (872). The degree to which we embrace intercession with persevering prayer will directly impact our family and our world.

Intercessory prayer heightens our awareness of the Holy Spirit who intercedes for us and guides us in knowing how to pray. Jesus said: **"I will ask the Father, and he will give you another Helper, who will stay with you forever. He is the Spirit who reveals the truth about God"** -John 14:16-17. **"In the same way the Spirit also comes to help us, weak as we are. For we do not know how we ought to pray; the Spirit himself pleads with God for us in groans that words cannot express. And God, who sees into our hearts, knows what the thought of the Spirit is; because the Spirit pleads with God on behalf of his people and in accordance with His will"** -Rom. 8:26-27. *Enthronement of the Image of the Divine Mercy* in the home helps us to avail ourselves of the graces of intercession in union with the one Mediator between God and man.

The recurring theme of the Passion of Christ, highlighted in the forms of the devotion, gives us the blueprint for deeper union with Christ and a life of intercessory prayer that will bear great fruit. Immersion in the Passion teaches us how to love God and souls (304). *"There is but one price at which souls are bought,"* Jesus said, *"and that is suffering united to My suffering on the cross."* (324). Our Lord, however, laments the fact that there are few who want to immerse themselves in the suffering side of the cross for the salvation of souls. *"I seek and desire souls like yours, but they are few. Your great trust in Me forces Me to continuously grant you graces"* (718).

Meditation on the Passion is the door into the Heart of Jesus. *"There is more merit to one hour of meditation on My sorrowful Passion"*, Jesus said, *"than there is to a whole year of flagellation that draws blood"* (369). Once in the Merciful Heart of Jesus, we become more like *The* intercessor, Jesus, who draws us into the mystery of Divine Mercy. Here, we find the safe refuge of the Sorrowful and Immaculate

Heart of Mary. Grace enables us to offer all our anxieties and sufferings to Jesus through Mary. Peace is the fruit of this offering to the Divine Will. Through grace we now learn to accept the trials and tribulations of our life within our family and our community in union with the sorrowful Mother Mary. *"...Although I was raised to the dignity of Mother of God,"* she said to Sister Faustina, *"seven swords of pain pierced My heart"* (786).

As intercessors, we are protected in the flames of love; our enemies cannot harm us (453). We come to understand the infinite love of Jesus for souls and are encouraged to enter into deeper intercession. At a deeper level of intercession we are called to surrender our family to the Merciful Jesus, trusting that their ultimate destiny is assured by Him, through our cooperation as intercessors. This grace may even extend to the complete surrender of our life and our possessions. We give all that Jesus desires so that His Will is accomplished; and He gives us the peace of resignation to His Will that comes from trust. *"We do not know the number of souls that are ours to save through our prayers and sacrifices;"* wrote Sister Faustina, *"therefore, let us always pray for sinners"* (1793).

IX. Enthronement of the Image of the Divine Mercy enlightens our mind and strengthens our will to uphold the sanctity of life.

"I want to pour out My divine life into human souls and sanctify them, if only they were willing to accept My grace...My kingdom on earth is my life in the human soul" (Diary, 1784)

The gift of Divine Mercy to the world today is overwhelming evidence of God's love for humanity. The image is a constant reminder that Jesus lay down His life for the salvation of each one of us. The wounds in His hands and feet and the rays pouring forth from His pierced Heart are the visible signs of our redemption. **"For God loved the world so much that He gave His only Son, so that everyone who believes in Him may not die but have eternal life. For God did not send His Son into the world to be its judge, but to be its Savior"** -John 3:16-17.

The world is not as powerful as it seems to be;" Jesus reminded Sister Faustina, *"its strength is strictly limited"* (1643). How consoling and encouraging these words are in the face of the culture of death. Evil darkens the mind and leads to confusion; whereas, the Image of the Divine Mercy, representing Christ, the light of the world, enlightens our mind and strengthens our will in the battle against the forces of evil. He said: **"I have come in order that you might have life-life in all its fullness"** -John 10:10. Jesus enables us to practice mercy toward our neighbor; to respect the dignity of each person we meet; to protect life in all its stages.

In the Diary of Sister Faustina we encounter ordinary people who were part of her daily life. As we enter into the mystery of His love and mercy through her experiences, we rediscover the infinite value of each soul in the eyes of God, especially those most in need of mercy. On several occasions, Sister Faustina endured horrendous suffering in reparation for the souls of babies who were aborted. Jesus gave her to understand that through her suffering she took part in His Agony in the Garden. She trembled with the very thought of this suffering, yet stressed her willingness to endure it to save one soul from such a fate (1276).

We know of Sister Faustina's great compassion and concern for the souls of her own earthly family, her community of sisters, the girls in their charge, her spiritual directors, priests and religious, her country, the souls in purgatory and for all mankind. In one very moving entry in her Diary, Sister asks Jesus to *"...look not on our sins, but on the tears of little children; on the hunger and cold they suffer. Jesus, for the sake of these innocent ones grant me the grace that I am asking of You for my country."* Jesus answered her: *"...what great compassion I have for them. Know that it is they who uphold the world (286).*

The witness of her life as a victim for souls reminds us, in these times of unspeakable crimes against life, of the dignity of each person, the sanctity of life and the Lord's desire that we be merciful at all times to all people. The challenge to exercise mercy must be answered today because of the sheer magnitude of evil perpetrated against individuals and peoples. We must not miss the point that **sins against the dignity of each person and sins against life itself are a reflection of the absence of mercy in man's soul.** The countless innocent unborn who are aborted, the defenseless children of the world who are neglected, abused and subjected to dastardly crimes, victims of violence, the poor, the sick and suffering, the hungry and homeless, the unemployed, prisoners, the lonely, the elderly and dying, sinners and those considered "useless" by our society, are not unlike the souls Sister Faustina helped through her charity, suffering and prayers.

It is an awesome challenge; yet, not an impossible task when we rely on the Merciful Jesus who wants to begin this task in our hearts and in our families. *Enthronement of the Image of the Divine Mercy and Consecration of the Family to God's Mercy* is a powerful way to touch the world with this fresh outpouring of Divine Mercy. It is mercy that enables us to understand the value of human life and the dignity of each person made in the image and likeness of God, especially those in our own family. It is mercy which is our defense. *"...Tell souls that I am giving them My mercy as a defense. I Myself am fighting for them and am bearing the just anger of My Father"* (1515). It is mercy which is our last hope. It is mercy we must embrace. *"Today,"* Sister Faustina wrote, *"I saw the glory of God which flows from the image. Many souls are receiving graces, although they do not speak of it openly. Even though it has met up with all sorts of vicissitudes, God is receiving glory because of it, and the efforts of Satan and of evil men are shattered and come to naught. In spite of Satan's anger, The Divine Mercy will triumph over the whole world and will be worshipped by all souls"* (1789).

Nine Graces of Enthronement
of the Image of
The Divine Mercy in the Home

1. *Welcomes* Jesus who enters our home and *becomes part of our family;*

2. *Raises* the soul to a higher degree of conversion and grace;

3. *Draws* us into the Paschal Mysteries as reflected in the image;

4. *Deepens* our love and understanding of the Sacraments of Mercy to heal, renew and transform our lives;

5. *Brings* Christ's peace to our home;

6. *Strengthens* our faith, *deepens* our trust and *increases* our love of God;

7. *Transforms* us into Apostles of Mercy in our families and in the world;

8. *Leads* us to a deeper life of intercessory prayer for our families and for the whole world;

9. *Enlightens* our mind and *strengthens* our will to uphold the sanctity of life.

CONCLUSION

In summary, our families need the powerful presence of Jesus to counteract the destructive influence of secularism. The enemies of the faith concentrate their attacks on the family, seeking to destroy the sacredness of the "domestic church." Their attacks are an attempt to negate the dignity of the family as modeled by the Holy Family of Nazareth. Jesus, as a member of a human family, recognized the necessity of bringing His healing presence into the home. *Enthronement of the Image of the Divine Mercy* in a home is an antidote to the kingdom of evil and sin. Jesus' mercy overpowers the kingdom of Satan. A family that consecrates its members and prays for God's mercy, enjoys the protection of Jesus Himself. His Divine Mercy penetrates and eradicates sinful attachments, selfishness and occult influences. Jesus said to Sister Faustina: *"I promise that the soul that will venerate this image will not perish. I also promise victory over its enemies already here on earth, especially at the hour of death. I Myself will defend it as My own glory"* (48).

The enthronement event gives the family the initial moment of grace whereby the home becomes the place of growth in the devotion to the Divine Mercy. The image is a reminder of Jesus' constant mercy and the assurance of our final salvation. Let us join together to blanket the earth with God's Mercy by *Enthroning His Image* in every church and home. This *is* the time of Divine Mercy.

Chapter 8

ENTHRONEMENT
OF
THE IMAGE OF THE DIVINE MERCY
IN THE HOME

Rite of Enthronement

and

Consecration

of

the Family

to

the Merciful Jesus

Rite of Enthronement

GREETING

Priest or Presider:

The enthronement ceremony exalts the Merciful Jesus, who said **"I Am King of Mercy,"** (88) honoring Him with a tenderness of heart. ***Enthronement of the Image of the Divine Mercy*** is a total commitment to the King of Mercy. It is an act of trust that speaks of our desire to receive as well as practice mercy, to forgive our enemies and those who have hurt us.

By Enthronement we claim our home for Jesus Christ, trusting in His Mercy to restore the dignity of the family and heal the brokenness in all families. Our commitment impacts the entire Body of Christ as we raise our voices in unison, "have mercy on us and on the whole world."

SCRIPTURE READING

Select one or two readings:

Luke 15:11-31   **(Parable of Divine Mercy)**
Romans 12:9-21 **(Fraternal Charity)**
Psalm 100   **(Thanksgiving)**

THE APOSTLES' CREED is recited as an act of faith in the teachings of Christ.

HOMILY OR TALK

A brief talk on the significance of the Divine Mercy coming into the home, the need to trust in God and the necessity of persevering prayer for the ongoing conversion of the family and the world.

When Jesus is enthroned as King of Mercy, our home becomes a fortress against the onslaughts of the enemies of the family and Christianity.

THE CHAPLET OF THE DIVINE MERCY

CONSECRATION TO THE MERCIFUL JESUS

CONCLUSION: Hail, Holy Queen, In honor of Mary, Mother of Mercy

Immaculate Heart of Mary, pray for us.
St. Joseph, pray for us.
Blessed Faustina, pray for us.

THE RITE OF ENTHRONEMENT

The rite or ceremony of *Enthronement of the Image of the Divine Mercy* consists in its presentation to a family by a priest,* his representative or a designated member of the family. The loving acceptance of Enthronement by the members of the family is reflected by an act of faith in the teachings of Jesus, who honors our family with His presence. This family event has a special religious significance for its members since it builds unity, faith and trust among them.

The image may be hung or placed on a stand in a prominent place, visible to all in the home.

The structure of the ceremony is based on the Word of God and emphasizes the commitment to Jesus in the act of consecration. The priest and the faithful pray together and learn about the Divine Mercy in an atmosphere of trust and love.

Flexibility and adaptability should help create an atmosphere where everyone feels as much at ease as they would if Jesus Himself were present. With the inspiration of the Holy Spirit, the family becomes more aware of the loving compassion of Jesus. Their joy in being with Him could be manifested with appropriate songs and hymns at the discretion of the leader.

GREETING

The priest, a designated representative or a member of the family addresses the group with these or similar words:

The enthronement ceremony exalts the Merciful Jesus, who said **"I Am King of Mercy,"** (88) honoring Him with a tenderness of heart. *Enthronement of the Image of the Divine Mercy* is a total commitment to the King of Mercy. It is an act of trust that speaks of our desire for reconciliation, healing and transformation.

By Enthronement we trust the Merciful Jesus to restore the dignity of the family and heal any brokenness in our family. Our commitment impacts the entire Body of Christ as we raise our voices in unison, "...have Mercy on us and on the whole world."

These words set the tone for the whole ceremony. The greeting may be brief but should contain the basic elements of the Enthronement: Honor to Jesus, the King of Mercy; a spirit of trust in Jesus' mercy; a willingness to give Him the first place in our homes and in our lives; a spirit of forgiveness; a desire to receive healing and experience the Peace of Christ in our hearts and in our homes; a commitment to exercise mercy toward our neighbor by deed, word and prayer.

SCRIPTURE READINGS

Jesus speaks to the family through His written word. Once the priest has selected the reading, a lector proclaims it to the group slowly and with devotion. The passages suggested are: the parable on Divine Mercy (Luke 15:11-31); St. Paul's passage on fraternal charity (Romans 12:9-21); or a psalm of Thanksgiving (Psalm 100). The priest is free to select any other reading that deals with the mercy of God and its practice such as the Sermon on the Mount.

THE APOSTLES' CREED

After the reading and meditation on the Word of God, the group recites the Apostles' Creed as an expression of faith. The priest might introduce it and lead it himself as an act of unity and faith in the teachings of Christ and loyalty to the Vicar of Christ, the Holy Father.

HOMILY OR TALK

The priest, or leader takes a few moments to exhort the group on the significance of the Divine Mercy in the home and the importance of prayer in the family. It is a moment of evangelization for all members of the family. Trust in God, the desire to receive as well as practice mercy and to forgive our enemies and those who have hurt us should be stressed. The home is claimed for Jesus Christ. With the help of Jesus' presence, it becomes a fortress against the attacks of the enemies of the family and the Christian faith. It is where Jesus brings *peace, healing and reconciliation*.

The talk should be short and presented with the same simplicity, compassion and understanding Jesus would use in speaking to us.

THE CHAPLET OF THE DIVINE MERCY

The prayerful recitation of the chaplet, mandated by Our Lord Himself, will prepare the family for the final Act of Consecration. In the chaplet, we offer to the Heavenly Father, the Person of the Son of God Incarnate. Invoking the sorrowful Passion of Jesus, each of us makes reparation for our sins and the sins of the whole world. The family also pleads for Jesus' Mercy which He wishes to bestow on them and on the whole world.

The recitation of the chaplet should be slow and meaningful in order to enter into the spirit of trust and reparation evoked by this prayer.

It is suggested that the priest begin the chaplet. Each decade may then be led by a different member of the family. If convenient it could be sung.

The Chaplet of the Divine Mercy is recited using ordinary rosary beads. Begin with: Our Father...Hail Mary...The Creed...

On the five large beads:
Eternal Father, I offer You the Body and Blood, Soul and Divinity of your dearly beloved Son, Our Lord Jesus Christ, in atonement for our sins and those of the whole world.

On the ten small beads:
For the sake of His sorrowful Passion, have mercy on us and on the whole world.

Conclude with (3 times): Holy God, Holy Mighty One, Holy Immortal One, have mercy on us and on the whole world.

---

* If a priest is not available to preside at the ceremony, the family may have the image blessed by a priest before the ceremony (if possible) or on Mercy Sunday. Many parishes have adapted the Rite of Enthronement for use in church. This encourages enthronement in homes. If the ceremony is held in a church, families are still encouraged to "enthrone" the Image of the Divine Mercy at home with family members present, if possible.

This is a very special moment for the family. Facing the image of Jesus, they may stand or kneel reverently while reciting the prayer of consecration with faith and trust.

Act of Consecration
of the Family to the Merciful Jesus

Almighty and Eternal Father, we, the (   ) family, *(each member of the family says his first name)*, consecrate ourselves and our home to Jesus, King of Mercy.

Merciful Jesus, we proclaim You King of Mercy and enthrone Your image in our home as an act of love and trust. It is our response to Your desire that souls know You as King of Mercy and venerate Your image as the Merciful Jesus throughout the world. May it be a constant reminder of Your Love and Mercy and Your promise to work in hearts that are open to You.

Strengthen our faith, *deepen* our trust and *increase* our love for You. *Draw us* into Your Merciful Heart, the source of our healing. *Help us* to trust in Your Goodness. *Give us* the grace to live in the present moment, with patience and resignation to Your Will, not dwelling on the past or living in fear of the future.

Heal the hurts and unforgiveness that prevent us from drawing closer to You. In Your mercy, help us to *reconcile* with You and with one another. *Transform us* so that we reflect Your mercy in our family, our community and our world by our actions, words and prayers. *Sanctify us* with Your Precious Blood and refresh us with the life-giving water which flowed from Your wounded Heart.

Come Holy Spirit, *teach, guide and inspire us* in these times of doubt and confusion. Give us *courage and perseverance* in prayer. We are confident that You are always with us and our family and that through this consecration You will bring the *Peace, Healing and Reconciliation* we need in our lives.

Come, Lord Jesus,
Renew our hearts, Restore our families. Amen.

Family members are invited to sign the consecration.

_____

_____

_____

(This consecration could be renewed once a week on Friday at the 3 o'clock Hour of Mercy or at a time convenient to the family).

CONCLUSION

In honor of the Blessed Mother, Queen and Mother of Mercy, the group fervently prays the HAIL, HOLY QUEEN. All join in imploring the intercession of Mary, Joseph and Blessed Faustina.

> Immaculate Heart of Mary, pray for us.
> Saint Joseph, pray for us.
> Blessed Faustina, pray for us.

The group may conclude with a hymn or song.

The merciful Heart of Jesus is now present in the family. True to His promise, the family enjoys the peace and love of the Savior who will continue to bless the family as it strives to grow closer to Him in the practice of Christian virtue.

EPILOGUE

Mary, Mother of the Enthronement

At the conclusion of this work on the *Enthronement of the Image of the Divine Mercy*, let us reflect on the place of Mary, the Mother of God, in this devotion. Some of the questions that may arise are: What is the relationship of Mary's Immaculate Heart to the enthronement of the Merciful Jesus in the home? Is it proper to speak of "enthroning Mary" in our home? What is the common ground that unites them?

In the present century humanity has received the explicit message of Mercy as the last hope for mankind. The *Enthronement of the Image of the Divine Mercy*, inspired by a revealed message to Blessed Faustina, proclaims **Jesus** as **King of Mercy** and **Mary** as **Mother of Mercy**. It is only one enthronement, that of Jesus, who is Mercy Itself. The connection between Jesus and Mary is real. It deals with the reality of the Love of God that came to us through His Son who become Man in the womb of the Blessed Mother. Before the state of humanity reaches chaotic proportions, Jesus wants to remind us that His infinite Mercy is still available to repentant humanity. Divine Mercy is the devotion for our times, our society, our Church and our families. It is the unifying force through which God reaches out to us in the Incarnation of His Son through the Blessed Mother.

The Second Vatican Council and the teachings of Pope John Paul II have pointed out that the mysteries of Christ are closely connected with those of His Mother Mary. We accept Mary as the Mother of Jesus and the Mother of Mercy, whose role is always to prepare and to lead us to Her Son, our Savior.

Our Catholic world at present struggles with a multiplicity and variety of popular Marian devotions, messages, visionaries, apparitions and pilgrim images. In spite of their basic spiritual appeal, they may have the effect of bombarding the senses and exposing the faithful to the dangers of pietism. When religious crusades take on a life of their own, they acquire a competitive spirit that may prompt some to seek personal advantage by manipulating the credulity and simplicity of undiscerning minds. The Kingdom of Jesus and the Queenship of Mary are reduced to a utilitarian dimension that is detrimental to the image of a God of love and mercy.

The *Enthronement of the Image of the Divine Mercy* honors the Person of Jesus Christ, the King of Mercy, the revelation of God's Merciful Love that endures for all ages. He is the only one adored and worshipped both in the Liturgy and in the private lives of all, in heaven and on earth. He must, therefore, have the primary place of honor in the home where the family gathers around His image to pay Him due homage and veneration. Jesus, Mercy Itself, shares the Merciful Love of the Father with each of the members of the family who accept Him with simplicity of heart and true humility.

By the act of enthronement the Love of God becomes real and is experienced by each member of the family according to his degree of willingness and repentance. It is the LOVE of Jesus that occupies the center of our lives. There are not two different hearts to be enthroned, that of Jesus and His Mother. It is only ONE LOVE - the Eternal Love of God the Father who created, redeemed and sanctifies us. Mary received this LOVE from the beginning when God prepared her, immaculate, full of His graces and endowed with His most precious gifts of nature and of grace, in order to become the seat of Wisdom, the womb of His mercy. It was in the womb that the Merciful Jesus received His own human heart. By conceiving through the power of the Holy Spirit, the body of Jesus was formed in Mary's body. His tiny heart began to beat at the rhythm of His mother's heart. It provided the point of contact between the eternal merciful love of God and the needed humanity. She was the sacred receptacle of Divine Mercy for us. Blessed Faustina wrote towards the end of her life:

You have indeed prepared a tabernacle for Yourself: the Blessed Virgin. Her immaculate Womb is your dwelling place, and the inconceivable miracle of Your mercy takes place, O Lord (1745).

We honor and venerate in the Heart of Jesus the same Love that God the Father has given Mary through eternity. He formed her heart to His own image of tenderness, sweetness and compassion. Jesus was born to a Mother who had a spotless heart, full of grace and also full of compassion, tenderness and sweetness. "O clemens, O pia, O dulcis Virgo Maria" we pray in the traditional "Hail Holy Queen."

The Heart of Mary remained immaculate and merciful because God made her to be the mother of "fairest love!" By enthroning the image of this Love we also enthrone the love which was present in the heart of His Mother.

There is a danger that many of today's Marian devotions and private messages become so concerned with defending a particular advocation of Mary, in a self-interested way, that they lose the proper focus of the devotion. The faithful are distracted from the fundamental unifying concept of the LOVE of God which should be the foundation of all devotion. Centering on the merciful and compassionate Love of Jesus who came to rescue the lost sheep, should give such Marian devotional practices the proper theological perspective. The Holy Spirit who made Mary capable of bringing to the world the Love of the Father, can cleanse and purify all the modern causes and their crusaders who might need purity of intention. There is ONE LORD, ONE MERCY.

God gives us His Mercy and compassion through His Son Jesus. It is in the Mercy of Jesus that we find the heart of His Mother. Jesus and Mary shared in the same merciful Love, that of the eternal Father. By enthroning Jesus, Mary is also "enthroned" at the same time, in our homes and in our lives.

Blessed Faustina learned to experience the mercy of Jesus by uniting herself with Mary, and by experiencing Her as a mother, a teacher and a guide. *"I am Mother to you all, thanks to the unfathomable Mercy of God"* (449).

As we enthrone the Merciful Jesus in our home, we also receive the presence of the Mother of Mercy who forms us in her Immaculate Heart enabling us to bring her healing love and mercy to others; who protects us against the attacks of the devil, who guides and leads us to the forgiveness of her Son, who shields the family with her mantle of blessings, who as a mother shares her Son's compassion and love for sinners. The traditional belief, "To Jesus through Mary," becomes particularly true in the *Enthronement of the Image of the Divine Mercy.*

In one of her visions Blessed Faustina saw her confessor kneeling at the feet of Mary and talking to Her. She said to him: *"I am not only Queen of heaven, but also Mother of Mercy and your mother,"* and she covered the priest with her mantle (330). Even if this applied to that particular priest, it can be said of all of us, her children, as we too are covered by the mantle of Mary which is a sign of her protective motherly love.

In the infinite mercy of God, we are given Jesus Christ as the King of Mercy who deserves the highest and first place of honor in our homes. Jesus accomplished the greatest act of Mercy on Calvary. It was at that solemn moment that Mary united her sufferings to His for our salvation and is given to us as our Mother. The merciful Father required of Mary at that moment, the same totality of Love as He required of His Son dying on the Cross. The Mother of Divine Love, was united with LOVE ITSELF at the supreme act of our Redemption.

If the mercy of Jesus, realized in the Passion and Death on the Cross, is signified in the image by the rays of mercy gushing forth from the Heart, we can also believe the rays of mercy are coming from Mary's pure heart offering herself for us. At one time, Blessed Faustina saw Mary appearing full of light, shedding her rays of mercy toward heaven above and toward earth below:

I saw the Mother of God, clothed in a bright robe, From Her Heart issued forth fiery rays, some of which were turned toward Heaven while the others were covering our country" (33).

On August 10, 1937, Blessed Faustina was inspired to write a poem on the Mother of God. In a poetic vein, Faustina wrote: *"O Mother Immaculate Virgin, in you the divine ray is reflected"* (1232).

There is no question that the divine rays of the merciful Jesus are shared by His Mother Mary. Shining with the light of Her Son, Mary helps us walk in the light of grace, dispelling the prince of darkness. When the family experiences the effects of the rays of mercy, Mary is there, acting with her graces, moving the repentant soul to receive Jesus. Mary's role is to intercede and help now and especially at the hour of our death. She brings the Light to the soul. When a family or an individual returns to God, the bright Morning Star shines in the darkened sky of the soul that is receiving healing and forgiveness from Jesus. The enthronement provides the occasion for the Mother to help the family to prepare to receive Jesus.

Once Jesus' presence is felt in the home, Mary remains as the Mother of the family praying and pleading for them. Her prayers extend to all and to the whole world. Mary encouraged Blessed Faustina to constantly plead for humanity like she does. *"Your lives must be like Mine; quiet and hidden in unceasing union with God, pleading for humanity and preparing the world for the second coming of God"* (625). As a Mother full of love, she wants to intercede for us and with us. She shares in the same Divine Mercy and desires to plead to her Son for all her children especially at this critical moment in the history of mankind.

Mary is the *Mother of the Enthronement* because God made her the Mother of humanity full of His Divine Love. In her, God provided the first home in the sacredness of her womb, and the first miracle of Mercy took place. When we enthrone the Image of Mercy, Mary also claims the family for Jesus and accepts it for her own. When Jesus takes possession of the home, Mary becomes its real Mother.

APPENDIX

Prayers

The Sign of the Cross

In the name of the Father, and of the Son, and of the Holy Spirit. Amen.

The Lord's Prayer

Our Father Who art in heaven, hallowed be Thy name; Thy kingdom come; Thy will be done on earth as it is in heaven. Give us this day our daily bread; and forgive us our trespasses as we forgive those who trespass against us; and lead us not into temptation, but deliver us from evil. Amen.

The Hail Mary

Hail, Mary, full of grace. The Lord is with thee; blessed art thou among women, and blessed is the fruit of thy womb, Jesus. Holy Mary, Mother of God, pray for us sinners now and at the hour of our death. Amen.

Glory be to the Father

Glory be to the Father, and to the Son, and to the Holy Spirit. As it was in the beginning, is now, and ever shall be forever. Amen.

The Apostles' Creed

I believe in God, the Father Almighty, Creator of heaven and earth; and in Jesus Christ, His only Son, Our Lord; who was conceived by the Holy Spirit, born of the Virgin Mary, suffered under Pontius Pilate, was crucified, died and was buried. He descended into hell; the third day He arose again from the dead; He ascended into heaven, sitteth at the right hand of God, the Father Almighty; from thence He shall come to judge the living and the dead.

I believe in the Holy Spirit, the Holy Catholic Church, the communion of saints, the forgiveness of sins, the resurrection of the body, and life everlasting. Amen.

Hail, Holy Queen

Hail, Holy Queen, Mother of mercy, hail, our life, our sweetness and our hope. To you do we cry, poor banished children of Eve. To you do we send up our sighs, mourning, and weeping in this vale of tears.

Turn then, most gracious advocate, your eyes of mercy toward us; and after this, our exile, show unto us the blessed fruit of your womb, Jesus! O clement, O loving, O sweet Virgin Mary!

Act of Spiritual Communion

My Jesus, I believe that You are present in the Blessed Sacrament. I love You above all things, and I long for You in my soul. Since I cannot now receive You sacramentally, come at least spiritually into my heart. I know You have already come. I embrace You and unite myself entirely to You; never permit me to be separated from You.

Chaplet of the Divine Mercy

(Recited using ordinary rosary beads)

Begin with: Our Father...Hail Mary...The Creed...

On the five large beads:
Eternal Father, I offer You the Body and Blood, Soul and Divinity of your dearly beloved Son, Our Lord Jesus Christ, in atonement for our sins and those of the whole world.

On the ten small beads:
For the sake of His sorrowful Passion, have mercy on us and on the whole world.

Conclude with (3 times): Holy God, Holy Mighty One, Holy Immortal One, have mercy on us and on the whole world.

Prayer for Healing

Jesus, may your pure and healthy blood circulate in my ailing organism, and may Your pure and healthy body transform my weak body, and may a healthy and vigorous life throb within me, if it is truly Your holy will (1089).

Sister Faustina

Be Apostles of Divine Mercy!

(Pope John Paul II)

We invite you to become part of this *New Apostolate of Mercy*. For information on our ministries of:

* **Enthronement of the Image of the Divine Mercy in the Home and the Act of Consecration of the Family to the Merciful Jesus;** *(the image used by our apostolate is a replica of the Cracow Image of the Divine Mercy reproduced from the negative given to us by the Congregation of the Sisters of Our Lady of Mercy in Poland for the work of Enthronement. It is one-of-a-kind and may be obtained through the apostolate).*

* **Priests of the Enthronement;**

* **The Divine Mercy Priests' Retreat Ministry;**

* **Family Renewal Ministry;**

* **Enrollment in the Apostolate and formation in the Spirituality of Peace Through Divine Mercy.**

Write to:

Peace Through Divine Mercy
25 Cambridge Avenue
Yonkers, New York 10707
Tel: (914) 337-0060   Fax: (914) 337-7028

The following may also be ordered from the Apostolate:
Reproductions of the Cracow Image of the
Divine Mercy
Blessed Faustina Prints
Our Lady of Guadalupe Prints
The Enthronement Package
Materials in the Spanish language are in preparation.

END NOTES

All Biblical quotations in this book are from *The New Catholic Study Bible*, St. Jerome Edition, Catholic Bible Press, 1985.

Diary of Sr. Faustina M. Kowalska, *Divine Mercy in My Soul,* copyright 1987. Congregation of Marians of the Immaculate Conception; all world rights reserved.

Chapter 3

Pope John Paul II, Visit to the Basilica of Our Lady of Guadalupe, Mexico City, January 27, 1979.

Pope John Paul II Beatification of Sr. Faustina: Homily, (St. Peter's Square, Rome, April 18, 1993).

Chapter 4

Kathleen Keefe, *"The First Priests' Retreat,"* The Voice of Padre Pio. Vol. XXIV, No. 12, 1994.

Padre Pio, Letters 1. These letters comprise the correspondence between Padre Pio and his spiritual directors.

Chapter 5

Pope John Paul II, *Mulieris Dignitatem. On the Dignity and Vocation of Women.* (Vatican City: Libreria Editrice Vaticano, 1988).